The
Complete Runner's
Day-by-Day
Log and Calendar
2008

The Complete Runner's Day-by-Day Log and Calendar 2008

MARTY JEROME

Random House
New York

Published in the United States by Random House, an imprint of The Random House
Publishing Group, a division of Random House, Inc., New York.

RANDOM HOUSE and colophon are registered trademarks of Random House, Inc.

ISBN: 978-1-4000-6340-6

www.atrandom.com

Printed in the United States of America on acid-free paper

2 4 6 8 9 7 5 3 1

FIRST EDITION

Designed by Carole Lowenstein

Introduction

Probably no one understands why you lace up your running shoes day after day. At least, they don't understand it with any certainty. The reasons you offer—fitness, stress management, a desire to win—may explain the tangible benefits, which are usually enough to quiet the people asking. But the very fact that you train also shows that, at some deep level, you believe you have control over your destiny, a faith that you can be better. One way or another, our training programs revolve around the power of change. Every workout gives us a reason to believe in it.

Most of us consider faith to play, at best, a passing role in our training. You need it at mile 20 of a marathon, when extra workouts haven't yielded better results, or when it's 36 degrees outside with a steady drizzle. Yet we also see faith exemplified in other runners. In those moments when you doubt your own abilities and dedication, here are five people who should give you a reason to believe.

In his moving autobiography, *This Voice in My Heart*, Gilbert Tuhabonye recounts his life as a world-class runner and survivor of a Burundi massacre. An ethnic Tutsi, Tuhabonye was a middle-distance champion by the time he reached high school, setting school records for both the 800 and 1500 meters. In October 1993, a coup ousted the Hutu president of his country. On the day of the putsch, a Hutu mob invaded Tuhabonye's high school and began hacking Tutsi students to death with machetes. The Hutus forced the rest into a building that was then set afire. Tuhabonye survived by lying under the bodies of the dead. When he finally made a run for the woods, his clothes were on fire. He expected the mob to give chase, but when they saw that he was burning, they let him go, assuming he would die. Tuhabonye made it to a hospital. After many months of painful recovery, he began to walk again, then to run.

He was an alternate for the Burundi Olympic team in the 1996 games, though he didn't get to compete. He eventually came to the United States, where he was an All-American runner and competed at the NCAA Championships for Abilene Christian University. Today, he and his wife and daughter live in Austin, Texas, where he works as a running coach for RunTex, an organization that, among other services, provides shoes, coaching, and events for at-risk individuals. He also heads Gilbert's Gazelles, a training program for distance runners of all types.

Tuhabonye often speaks at churches and to youth groups (with encouragement from Texas governor Rick Perry). He carries the obvious message that running can change your life; it can also occasionally *save* your life. Where a runner's faith is concerned, changing lives and saving lives are often indistinguishable.

Even better is the belief that cheating isn't the only path to success. As the doping scandals continue to tarnish track-and-field events around the world, a new generation of American runners is proving that talent and hard work are sufficient for victory. While her teammates were suspended for failing drug tests,

21-year-old Lauryn Williams stepped forward to win a silver medal at the 2004 Olympic Games in Athens. She ran a poised and confident race. Since then, she has won the World Outdoor 100 meters, the World Outdoor 4 × 100–meter relay, and the silver medal for the World Indoor 100 meters. She is one of the fastest human beings in the world today.

Williams discovered her love for racing when she was 10, by racing Florence Griffith-Joyner—or at least by racing an avatar of the now deceased legend. One bright Saturday morning, her father took her to an exhibit at the Carnegie Science Center in Pittsburgh, which invited attendees to race down a 10-meter track against an electronic silhouette of Griffith-Joyner. Williams immediately lost interest in everything else the center offered. She raced the flashing image from late morning until late afternoon before finally beating it. She was hooked.

Though she was competitive in a variety of sports as a young girl, Williams loved to race first and foremost. Her mother recalls that she beat all the girls in the neighborhood, and then she beat all the boys. She earned her degree at the University of Miami in three and a half years, while winning the NCAA title in the 100 meters. At the Olympic trials in Sacramento, Williams faced two racing Goliaths: Marion Jones and Gail Devers. She beat them both, winning a spot on the team. This kind of competitive drive has led countless runners into the self-defeating temptations of performance drugs. Not Williams, who is even afraid to take multivitamins for what they may do to her drug tests. "I want to be 100 percent me," she says. Is there a better mantra for any runner?

Young athletes never escape the media spotlight, of course. Yet runners over 40 make up the fastest-growing segment of the sport. Ed Whitlock's latest marathon time was 2:54, a fine performance for any average amateur distance runner. What sets Whitlock apart is that he was 73 years old when he crossed the finish line, leaving slack-jawed 25-year-olds in his dust. The septuagenarian has set world records for his age category in every distance event from the 5K to the marathon. Sports physiologists are fascinated by him. Runners everywhere wonder if he overturns conventional wisdom about aging.

The silver-haired Canadian doesn't eat a special diet. He doesn't cross train or work with coaches. He doesn't even log the distances he runs. After toast and several cups of tea each morning, he simply begins running—three hours a day, in a loop around a neighborhood cemetery. The only speed work he does comes from the 35 races he typically enters each year. If there's any secret to Whitlock's training, it's that he continues to increase the hours he trains as he ages.

Even Whitlock agrees that he can't train at his current intensity forever. Meanwhile, science is barely catching up to the man. The most comprehensive study of the aging human heart affirms only now that older athletes can achieve more fitness gains than previously thought. In fact, Benjamin D. Levine, a cardiologist and an author of the study, found that people who began exercising in midlife and kept it up had hearts that were indistinguishable from those of healthy 30-year-olds. What scientists can't explain is the gratification and private faith that keep runners training into the winter of their lives.

Unfortunately, not all of us will make it to winter. As often as not, a toss of the dice decides who will. Ronni Gordon, a 48-year-old reporter for *The Republican*, in Springfield, Massachusetts, felt fine when the starting gun sounded at a 10K race on St. Patrick's Day in 2003. Soon afterward, she felt unaccountably out of breath and exhausted, barely able to complete the event. Her time to the finish line jumped by 10 minutes. This was unusual for someone who routinely ran 20 miles a week and played on a tennis team. So the single mother of three saw a doctor, who gave her a shocker: acute myeloid leukemia, a fast-moving cancer that could be fatal within months. Had she not raced that fateful day, her symptoms might have proceeded undetected until it was too late.

Gordon immediately began a grueling six-month series of chemotherapy sessions, often spending five or more days at a time in the hospital, with weeks recuperating at home in between. Her hair fell out, grew back, then fell out again. At one point she developed pneumonia that required lung surgery. Spiking fevers, diarrhea, and head-to-toe rashes were so bad that she often couldn't eat and wanted only to curl up in bed. But she also knew that any exercise at all would give her energy and a sense of accomplishment.

She began with small goals—walking up and down a corridor in the hospital, dragging her IV stand—"putting one foot in front of the other," as she says. When she came home for good, she had endured the third and most potent round of chemotherapy, along with a stem-cell transplant to regenerate her depleted bone marrow. She could barely walk up a short hill. Soon afterward, she began walking again, then jogging at a local track. A little more than a year after she returned home from her last round of chemo, she ran her first six-mile race, still putting one foot in front of the other and recognizing that, at least for the moment, she had her life back.

A runner's faith doesn't always yield results in expected ways. In addition to his New York City Marathon number, Jim Deupree has a number that identifies him as a convict in the Florida state prison system, where he is currently serving a 30-year sentence for armed robbery. He doesn't dispute his conviction. And no, he won't be running through the boroughs of New York anytime soon. But in 2005, he petitioned the New York Road Runners, which organizes the marathon, to run the race by proxy from a dirt track in his prison yard, which measures 2.25 laps to the mile. His stated purpose was to raise money for cancer research in memory of George Sheehan, the late running writer, who had sent Deupree occasional encouraging letters (and less occasionally, free running shoes). The Road Runners granted the 69-year-old convict a race number.

Did he actually complete the marathon? No one will confirm it, not even prison officials, who seem warily contemptuous of the whole affair. This is probably because it wasn't the first time Deupree ran a race by proxy. As to the money he purportedly raised for cancer research, the amount and the names of the receiving organizations are vague at best. Deupree's personal history, as those of many prisoners, is filled with self-defeating poor judgment that has led him into a perpetual cha-cha dance between the street and the slammer. In fact, it's quite possible that Jim Deupree is just another flimflam artist who managed to con an elite running organization into free publicity.

Among the facts we know: When he first entered prison, he stood five foot nine and weighed 250 pounds. He began running and lost 50 pounds. When he was released in 1979, he ran 269 miles from the prison gates to his home in Shelbyville, Indiana, over 12 days, which attracted a lot of publicity. He's been re-arrested since, yet he continues to run, his weight down to well under 170. The free running shoes no longer arrive at his prison cell. The hopeful publicity is gone. Yet still Deupree runs. All of us make poor and fateful decisions in our lives, and it's a miracle that we learn from them. Jim Deupree won't find redemption in the miles he logs. But as with the rest of us, running gives him a way to hold on to whatever freedom he can.

The
Complete Runner's Day-by-Day Log and Calendar
2008

JANUARY

S	M	T	W	T	F	S
		1 NEW YEAR'S DAY	2	3	4	5
6	7	8	9	10	11	12
13	14	15	16	17	18	19
20	21 MARTIN LUTHER KING, JR., DAY	22	23	24	25	26
27	28	29	30	31		

January: Desire

You probably know to be careful about what you wish for in love, work, and children. These answered prayers have a habit of biting you in the rump. Too often we make the same mistake when setting goals for our training programs. Through folly, blind hope, or some unrealistic desire, we sabotage ourselves by aiming for the wrong things.

You can see how this happens when your running program comes up for review. The New Year, with its solemn resolutions, makes an auspicious time to reassess, especially because it urges us to reflect on what's possible and, more significant, on what brings us joy in running. Yet often this is the only time we reexamine our goals—the first mistake. Two better occasions: after a success and after a failure. Both experiences are loaded with information. Both provide a hard reality check. Take advantage of them, whenever they occur on the calendar.

Another self-sabotaging mistake is to set goals according to ends rather than means. This is counterintuitive, since the word *goal*, after all, implies accomplishment. But when the Maui Marathon is circled as your goal, illness or schedule conflicts can intervene. Results fail to materialize. You're less likely to fail if you establish weekly and monthly mileage objectives that will prepare you for the marathon, regardless of whether or not you run it. You have more control over these factors. The same is true of weight-loss and speed goals. Focus on the frequency and types of workouts that let you shed pounds or seconds. The end results will take care of themselves.

By the way, if it can't be measured, it's not a goal. A New Year's resolution to "run more days during the week" is a prayer of good intentions that is up for negotiation on every icy morning that you glance at your running shoes. A resolution to "log 30 miles a week," however, requires a commitment and a plan. It imposes the kind of discipline that keeps any training program vital.

While discipline matters, joy and exuberance keep us running. These blessings are also fraught. It may surprise you, but the fitter you are, the less room you have to improve. It's a cruel twist—often overlooked—but just as you reach the peak of physical condition, you'll actually have to lower your aspirations, or change them, anyway; as with the realities of aging, this means looking for gratification in other ways. Facing limits is an important life skill. Get used to it.

Joy and exuberance also fail to take into account your history as a runner. Past accomplishments (and failures) must inform the goals you set for the New Year, but they shouldn't become a tyranny. The miracle of running is that with each workout, each step, you are becoming a different person—stronger, certainly, but also more invested in life and the possibilities it holds. Imagination and desire should drive your goals as a runner. They should drive your goals as a human being. Let them run wild.

*"A pat on the back is only a few vertebrae from a kick in the pants—
but is miles ahead in results."*   —ELLA WHEELER WILCOX, AMERICAN POET

MONDAY, DECEMBER 31   365

WHERE & WHEN _____ DISTANCE _____
COMMENTS _____

TUESDAY, JANUARY 1   1

WHERE & WHEN _____ DISTANCE _____
COMMENTS _____

WEDNESDAY, JANUARY 2   2

WHERE & WHEN _____ DISTANCE _____
COMMENTS _____

THURSDAY, JANUARY 3   3

WHERE & WHEN _____ DISTANCE _____
COMMENTS _____

FRIDAY, JANUARY 4   4

WHERE & WHEN _____ DISTANCE _____
COMMENTS _____

SATURDAY, JANUARY 5

WHERE & WHEN _____ DISTANCE _____
COMMENTS _____

SUNDAY, JANUARY 6

WHERE & WHEN _____ DISTANCE _____
COMMENTS _____

Buy smaller dishes if you're trying to control meal portions.
The typical plate in Europe is 9 inches; in America, it's
11 inches—or 30 percent larger.

"Believe in yourself, know yourself, deny yourself, and be humble."
—JOHN TREACY, ON THE FOUR PRINCIPLES OF RACING

MONDAY, JANUARY 7   7

WHERE & WHEN _____ DISTANCE _____
COMMENTS _____

TUESDAY, JANUARY 8   8

WHERE & WHEN _____ DISTANCE _____
COMMENTS _____

WEDNESDAY, JANUARY 9   9

WHERE & WHEN _____ DISTANCE _____
COMMENTS _____

THURSDAY, JANUARY 10   10

WHERE & WHEN _____ DISTANCE _____
COMMENTS _____

FRIDAY, JANUARY 11   11

WHERE & WHEN _____ DISTANCE _____
COMMENTS _____

SATURDAY, JANUARY 12

12

WHERE & WHEN _____ DISTANCE _____
COMMENTS _____

SUNDAY, JANUARY 13

13

WHERE & WHEN _____ DISTANCE _____
COMMENTS _____

To get faster, don't increase your stride at all; concentrate on
a faster turnover rate instead.

DISTANCE THIS WEEK_____ WEIGHT_____

"In a country where only men are encouraged, one must be one's own inspiration."

—TEGLA LOROUPE, KENYA, 1994 NEW YORK CITY MARATHON CHAMPION

MONDAY, JANUARY 14   14

WHERE & WHEN _____ DISTANCE _____
COMMENTS _____

TUESDAY, JANUARY 15   15

WHERE & WHEN _____ DISTANCE _____
COMMENTS _____

WEDNESDAY, JANUARY 16   16

WHERE & WHEN _____ DISTANCE _____
COMMENTS _____

THURSDAY, JANUARY 17   17

WHERE & WHEN _____ DISTANCE _____
COMMENTS _____

FRIDAY, JANUARY 18   18

WHERE & WHEN _____ DISTANCE _____
COMMENTS _____

SATURDAY, JANUARY 19

WHERE & WHEN _____ DISTANCE _____
COMMENTS _____

SUNDAY, JANUARY 20

WHERE & WHEN _____ DISTANCE _____
COMMENTS _____

DISTANCE THIS WEEK_____ WEIGHT_____

"I will keep on going as long as the legs keep moving."
—JENNY WOOD ALLEN, AFTER COMPLETING A MARATHON AT 91 YEARS OF AGE

MONDAY, JANUARY 21   21

WHERE & WHEN _____ DISTANCE _____
COMMENTS _____

TUESDAY, JANUARY 22   22

WHERE & WHEN _____ DISTANCE _____
COMMENTS _____

WEDNESDAY, JANUARY 23   23

WHERE & WHEN _____ DISTANCE _____
COMMENTS _____

THURSDAY, JANUARY 24   24

WHERE & WHEN _____ DISTANCE _____
COMMENTS _____

FRIDAY, JANUARY 25   25

WHERE & WHEN _____ DISTANCE _____
COMMENTS _____

SATURDAY, JANUARY 26

26

WHERE & WHEN _____ DISTANCE _____

COMMENTS _____

SUNDAY, JANUARY 27

27

WHERE & WHEN _____ DISTANCE _____

COMMENTS _____

When returning from an injury, add no more than 10 percent
a week to your mileage.

FEBRUARY

S	M	T	W	T	F	S
					1	2
3	4	5	6 ASH WEDNESDAY	7	8	9
10	11	12 LINCOLN'S BIRTHDAY	13	14 VALENTINE'S DAY	15	16
17	18 PRESIDENTS' DAY	19	20	21	22 WASHINGTON'S BIRTHDAY	23
24	25	26	27	28	29	

February: Passion

If you were given a choice, you probably wouldn't give up your house or your children for the privilege of running, though there are days when this surely seems tempting. Could you give up ice cream? Would you forgo your rent-controlled apartment or the memory of your first kiss—if it meant that you could work out whenever you wanted, anytime you felt the urge to put on your running shoes?

Olympians and high school track stars don't trouble themselves with these hypothetical trifles. They'd give up practically anything for training because it's the proven window to victory. The rest of us have to juggle conflicting goals, demanding schedules, and our changing desires and abilities. Even so, it's passion that motivates both the Olympic champion and the weekend jogger. Even if our fervor is nothing more than the love for a solitary hour on the open road, its importance is transcendent.

Passion for running can be treacherous, however. It often distorts judgment. You'll find yourself on the starting line of a race you're not quite prepared to run. You'll push recuperation from the flu by a couple of days, believing that a light workout will clear your head and lungs. You'll add extra hill charges, because you can't resist the exhilaration, the sweet depletion you feel during the recovery phase. Six miles into your customary run, you'll suddenly remember that you were supposed to meet your boss for dinner an hour ago.

Passion can also betray you in the ways it ebbs over time. Many runners easily rekindle excitement for their city's annual marathon or for a 10K fund-raiser. The workouts leading up to these events teem with memories of past achievements and the tribal fun that comes with competition. But notice how passion sags in the long training periods between events. Likewise, noncompetitive runners still get satisfaction when they glimpse their figures in the mirror years after they began running. There's still a thrill in strength—whether it's felt when passing a younger runner on a wide outside bend or simply in the pleasing stretch of your calf muscles while ascending a flight of stairs. Yet do these moments provide sufficient motivation for a workout when it's 36 degrees and rainy?

In one way or another, we all struggle to keep our passion for running alive, at the very least by keeping it new: changing the places and distances we run, adding interval training or trail workouts, signing up for competitive events that promise new challenges. We shake it up. These changes to our routines help us become better runners. They reveal new strengths and weaknesses. They develop muscles and skills that otherwise tend to atrophy.

But novelty alone won't keep passion burning; after all, consistency and persistence are the pathways to improvement. Running is first and foremost the love of a habit, of putting one foot in front of the other. A good training program helps us find new ways to enjoy familiar routines. It promises nothing more than improvement. It knows that passion will take care of itself.

"Hard things take time to do. Impossible things take a little longer."
—PERCY CERUTTY, LEGENDARY AUSTRALIAN RUNNING COACH

MONDAY, JANUARY 28   28

WHERE & WHEN _____ DISTANCE _____
COMMENTS _____

TUESDAY, JANUARY 29   29

WHERE & WHEN _____ DISTANCE _____
COMMENTS _____

WEDNESDAY, JANUARY 30   30

WHERE & WHEN _____ DISTANCE _____
COMMENTS _____

THURSDAY, JANUARY 31   31

WHERE & WHEN _____ DISTANCE _____
COMMENTS _____

FRIDAY, FEBRUARY 1   32

WHERE & WHEN _____ DISTANCE _____
COMMENTS _____

SATURDAY, FEBRUARY 2   33

WHERE & WHEN _____ DISTANCE _____
COMMENTS _____

SUNDAY, FEBRUARY 3   34

WHERE & WHEN _____ DISTANCE _____
COMMENTS _____

Losing your fitness happens shockingly fast. Even 30 minutes
of light aerobic activity three times a week can slow
that deterioration to a crawl.

DISTANCE THIS WEEK _____ WEIGHT _____

"No matter how many years you've been running, the hardest part is always taking that first step out the door."
—JOHN STRUMSKY, PRESIDENT OF THE U.S. RUNNING STREAK ASSOCIATION

MONDAY, FEBRUARY 4   35

WHERE & WHEN _____ DISTANCE _____
COMMENTS _____

TUESDAY, FEBRUARY 5   36

WHERE & WHEN _____ DISTANCE _____
COMMENTS _____

WEDNESDAY, FEBRUARY 6   37

WHERE & WHEN _____ DISTANCE _____
COMMENTS _____

THURSDAY, FEBRUARY 7   38

WHERE & WHEN _____ DISTANCE _____
COMMENTS _____

FRIDAY, FEBRUARY 8   39

WHERE & WHEN _____ DISTANCE _____
COMMENTS _____

WHERE & WHEN _____ DISTANCE _____

COMMENTS _____

WHERE & WHEN _____ DISTANCE _____

COMMENTS _____

Is it possible that two identical pairs of shoes (same models and sizes) can fit differently? Yes—you should try on both of them before you buy.

"The difference between the mile and the marathon is the difference between burning your fingers with a match and being slowly roasted over hot coals." —HAL HIGDON, *ON THE RUN FROM DOGS AND PEOPLE*

MONDAY, FEBRUARY 11   42

WHERE & WHEN _____ DISTANCE _____
COMMENTS _____

TUESDAY, FEBRUARY 12   43

WHERE & WHEN _____ DISTANCE _____
COMMENTS _____

WEDNESDAY, FEBRUARY 13   44

WHERE & WHEN _____ DISTANCE _____
COMMENTS _____

THURSDAY, FEBRUARY 14   45

WHERE & WHEN _____ DISTANCE _____
COMMENTS _____

FRIDAY, FEBRUARY 15   46

WHERE & WHEN _____ DISTANCE _____
COMMENTS _____

WHERE & WHEN _____ DISTANCE _____
COMMENTS _____

WHERE & WHEN _____ DISTANCE _____
COMMENTS _____

"If I faltered, there would be no arms to hold me, and the world would be a cold and forbidding place." —SIR ROGER BANNISTER

MONDAY, FEBRUARY 18   49

WHERE & WHEN _____ DISTANCE _____
COMMENTS _____

TUESDAY, FEBRUARY 19   50

WHERE & WHEN _____ DISTANCE _____
COMMENTS _____

WEDNESDAY, FEBRUARY 20   51

WHERE & WHEN _____ DISTANCE _____
COMMENTS _____

THURSDAY, FEBRUARY 21   52

WHERE & WHEN _____ DISTANCE _____
COMMENTS _____

FRIDAY, FEBRUARY 22   53

WHERE & WHEN _____ DISTANCE _____
COMMENTS _____

WHERE & WHEN _____ DISTANCE _____

COMMENTS _____

SUNDAY, FEBRUARY 24

55

WHERE & WHEN _____ DISTANCE _____

COMMENTS _____

Feel like skipping a workout? Go for a 10-minute jog instead,
with the intention of quitting at any point after that. Almost
invariably, you'll finish your customary distance.

DISTANCE THIS WEEK _____ WEIGHT _____

MARCH

S	M	T	W	T	F	S
						1
2	3	4	5	6	7	8
9	10	11	12	13	14	15
16 PALM SUNDAY	17 ST. PATRICK'S DAY	18	19	20	21 GOOD FRIDAY	22
23 EASTER	24	25	26	27	28	29
30	31					

March: Morals

After their fabled race, the tortoise should have invited the hare out for a beer. The hare's secrets for speed would benefit any running program, even if speed is beside the point. The moral to their tale is actually the opposite of what most of us learned in childhood: endurance training, rather than sprints, invites complacency.

Speed work bestows efficiency on your workouts, building strength and improving your body's oxygen uptake with fewer miles of effort. It helps you maintain your pace and form during the last 20 percent of a long run, whether it's a race or a workout. It sheds new light on your shortcomings as a runner. And it shakes a training program out of tedium, trading plodding routine for bursts of exhilaration.

The question for distance runners is how to get the most from speed work, especially if you hate it. By the way, it's okay to hate it, at least initially. In fact, the best way to introduce it into your workouts is by coyly playing with it: on your next customary long run, put on a sustained surge that's only moderately faster than your normal pace. Hold this quicker tempo just until you begin to feel winded, which tells you that you've switched into an anaerobic burn. Now slow down until you recover. Repeat. This is your basic interval—no need for stopwatches, coaches, or programmatic workouts. When you're new to intervals, the number you add to your workouts is more important than the speed at which you run them. By the way, give yourself at least one day of rest or cross training between these workouts.

You'll see results within weeks. And if you're like most runners, you'll also find new gratification in your training. Intervals are touchstones for change; almost miraculously, a better runner emerges, exuding new confidence and agility.

Once you're hooked on the benefits of speed work, you'll want to direct your efforts toward specific goals. So bring on the stopwatches and checklists. The Internet teems with workouts and advice. Don't expect to find much consensus about how to get the most from intervals, however. Running coaches prescribe tailored workouts with the solemn faith of witch doctors. Controversy has swirled around the subject since the end of World War II. The best we know from sports physiology is that "maximal" intervals—very fast repeats, of two to ten minutes each—yield the best results for most endurance athletes.

As the hare understood, speed is a seductive path to the finish line, which is why it invites hubris. You should begin interval training with the recognition that the benefits eventually peak and that if you keep pushing to squeeze out ever more performance, you risk disappointment or injury. Likewise, your body requires far more rest between interval workouts than it needs for your weekly long run. A little-known secret is that the hare's dillydallying between sprints wasn't because of arrogance. It was because his legs were tired.

"Running is the greatest metaphor for life, because you get out of it what you put into it."
—OPRAH WINFREY

MONDAY, FEBRUARY 25   56

_____
_____
_____
_____

WHERE & WHEN _____ DISTANCE _____
COMMENTS _____
_____

TUESDAY, FEBRUARY 26   57

_____
_____
_____
_____

WHERE & WHEN _____ DISTANCE _____
COMMENTS _____
_____

WEDNESDAY, FEBRUARY 27   58

_____
_____
_____
_____

WHERE & WHEN _____ DISTANCE _____
COMMENTS _____
_____

THURSDAY, FEBRUARY 28   59

_____
_____
_____
_____

WHERE & WHEN _____ DISTANCE _____
COMMENTS _____
_____

FRIDAY, FEBRUARY 29   60

_____
_____
_____
_____

WHERE & WHEN _____ DISTANCE _____
COMMENTS _____
_____

SATURDAY, MARCH 1 61

WHERE & WHEN _____ DISTANCE _____
COMMENTS _____

SUNDAY, MARCH 2 62

WHERE & WHEN _____ DISTANCE _____
COMMENTS _____

Supercushioned running shoes absorb shock and reduce
injury on long runs. But for speed work, consider using a
lighter pair.

"Success is a journey, not a destination. The doing is usually more important than the outcome."
—ARTHUR ASHE

MONDAY, MARCH 3   63

WHERE & WHEN _____ DISTANCE _____
COMMENTS _____

TUESDAY, MARCH 4   64

WHERE & WHEN _____ DISTANCE _____
COMMENTS _____

WEDNESDAY, MARCH 5   65

WHERE & WHEN _____ DISTANCE _____
COMMENTS _____

THURSDAY, MARCH 6   66

WHERE & WHEN _____ DISTANCE _____
COMMENTS _____

FRIDAY, MARCH 7   67

WHERE & WHEN _____ DISTANCE _____
COMMENTS _____

SATURDAY, MARCH 8

WHERE & WHEN _____ DISTANCE _____

COMMENTS _____

SUNDAY, MARCH 9

WHERE & WHEN _____ DISTANCE _____

COMMENTS _____

DISTANCE THIS WEEK_____ WEIGHT_____

"If you go out knowing you will never give up, you'll still lose most of the time, but you'll be in the best position to kick on that rare day when everything breaks right." —BILL BOWERMAN, FOUNDER OF NIKE

MONDAY, MARCH 10   70

WHERE & WHEN _____ DISTANCE _____
COMMENTS _____

TUESDAY, MARCH 11   71

WHERE & WHEN _____ DISTANCE _____
COMMENTS _____

WEDNESDAY, MARCH 12   72

WHERE & WHEN _____ DISTANCE _____
COMMENTS _____

THURSDAY, MARCH 13   73

WHERE & WHEN _____ DISTANCE _____
COMMENTS _____

FRIDAY, MARCH 14   74

WHERE & WHEN _____ DISTANCE _____
COMMENTS _____

WHERE & WHEN _____ DISTANCE _____
COMMENTS _____

SUNDAY, MARCH 16   76

WHERE & WHEN _____ DISTANCE _____
COMMENTS _____

After a hard workout, bring on the high-glycemic-index
foods—bagels, oatmeal, mashed potatoes, pasta, and the like.
They'll help you recover more quickly.

"Continuous effort—not strength or intelligence—is the key to unlocking our potential."
—LIANE CARDES, AUTHOR

MONDAY, MARCH 17   77

WHERE & WHEN _____ DISTANCE _____
COMMENTS _____

TUESDAY, MARCH 18   78

WHERE & WHEN _____ DISTANCE _____
COMMENTS _____

WEDNESDAY, MARCH 19   79

WHERE & WHEN _____ DISTANCE _____
COMMENTS _____

THURSDAY, MARCH 20   80

WHERE & WHEN _____ DISTANCE _____
COMMENTS _____

FRIDAY, MARCH 21   81

WHERE & WHEN _____ DISTANCE _____
COMMENTS _____

SATURDAY, MARCH 22

WHERE & WHEN _____ DISTANCE _____
COMMENTS _____

SUNDAY, MARCH 23

WHERE & WHEN _____ DISTANCE _____
COMMENTS _____

DISTANCE THIS WEEK _____ WEIGHT_____

"Write your goal down and post it on your refrigerator or bathroom mirror or in a drawer at work. Whenever you see the piece of paper, it will help you refocus." —DEENA KASTOR, 2004 OLYMPIC MARATHONER

MONDAY, MARCH 24   84

_____
_____
_____
_____

WHERE & WHEN _____ DISTANCE _____
COMMENTS _____
_____

TUESDAY, MARCH 25   85

_____
_____
_____
_____

WHERE & WHEN _____ DISTANCE _____
COMMENTS _____
_____

WEDNESDAY, MARCH 26   86

_____
_____
_____
_____

WHERE & WHEN _____ DISTANCE _____
COMMENTS _____
_____

THURSDAY, MARCH 27   87

_____
_____
_____
_____

WHERE & WHEN _____ DISTANCE _____
COMMENTS _____
_____

FRIDAY, MARCH 28   88

_____
_____
_____
_____

WHERE & WHEN _____ DISTANCE _____
COMMENTS _____
_____

WHERE & WHEN _____ DISTANCE _____

COMMENTS _____

WHERE & WHEN _____ DISTANCE _____

COMMENTS _____

Flat feet and fallen arches are the culprit of much back pain.
Make sure you're running in proper shoes and that you have
strong feet (while standing, pick up a pencil with your toes;
20 reps each foot).

DISTANCE THIS WEEK_____ WEIGHT_____

APRIL

S	M	T	W	T	F	S
		1	2	3	4	5
6	7	8	9	10	11	12
13	14	15	16	17	18	19
20 PASSOVER	21	22	23	24	25	26
27	28	29	30			

April: Comeback

Illness and injury strike most runners as a betrayal in much the way an unfaithful lover does. When shock and anger subside, we're left with lingering depression and impatience with the whole tawdry business.

Impatience is dangerous—even more so for older runners and for those who have been sidelined longer than a few months. The first rule in making a comeback is to lose all timelines for recovery, including race dates; strike them from your calendar until you feel the progress of rehab. Let your body alone guide the pace of that progress. And listen to it with the skepticism of a jilted lover. Even one overoptimistic workout can set you back weeks.

Speaking of setbacks, count on them. Injury in particular has the cruel proclivity of reasserting itself suddenly and seemingly without provocation. It will force you to dial back your workouts to unsatisfactory low-effort slogs, dutifully pounding them out for weeks, even months, with the dread that the viper could strike again. Remind yourself that even when you're in peak condition, progress isn't linear. You have to work through setbacks and plateaus in your body's own time. When you're making a comeback, these workout limbos simply last longer and occur more frequently.

If this sounds demoralizing, seek help from others—and be resourceful about it. With recurring injuries, for example, consider bypassing your family doctor for a sports medicine clinic, many of which will prescribe specific workouts in addition to conventional remedies. An experienced running coach can often identify problems in your form that cause pain and injury and also suggest how to make your workouts more efficient. A couple of sessions with a coach can be money well spent. And if you've been a snob about running partners or clubs, perhaps it's time for a little humility. A comeback tends to be slow and depressing. The moral support from a group or a partner can open new windows on your workouts and your goals. Besides, it's not a marriage; if partners become too competitive or dilatory, you're free to leave.

Cross training can likewise shore up morale. Weights and resistance training build core strength, which is invaluable to any runner and which tends to get shoved aside as endurance and speed goals fire the imagination. Core strength speeds recovery. Cardio exercises—swimming, aerobics, using elliptical trainers, or any routine that sustains a higher heart rate—will rebuild your base as you wait for your body to mend. Together, these drills also keep your weight in check.

There's yet another reason that cross training is useful. In one way or another, you will return from illness or injury a changed runner. Will you ever be as fast again? Will there be another marathon in your future? Questions like these can haunt you for months after you've recovered. Make a promise to live gracefully with these insecurities. Most old strengths eventually return; new strengths and abilities will reveal themselves over time. Cross training presents a marvelous way to explore what's lost and gained in the bargain. It's a great way to meet the new you.

"Any runner who denies having fears, nerves, or some kind of disposition is a bad athlete or a liar."
—GORDON PIRIE, 1956 OLYMPIC BRONZE-MEDAL WINNER FOR MEN'S 5000 METERS

MONDAY, MARCH 31   91

WHERE & WHEN _____ DISTANCE _____
COMMENTS _____

TUESDAY, APRIL 1   92

WHERE & WHEN _____ DISTANCE _____
COMMENTS _____

WEDNESDAY, APRIL 2   93

WHERE & WHEN _____ DISTANCE _____
COMMENTS _____

THURSDAY, APRIL 3   94

WHERE & WHEN _____ DISTANCE _____
COMMENTS _____

FRIDAY, APRIL 4   95

WHERE & WHEN _____ DISTANCE _____
COMMENTS _____

WHERE & WHEN _____ DISTANCE _____

COMMENTS _____

WHERE & WHEN _____ DISTANCE _____

COMMENTS _____

Stretching shouldn't hurt. If it does, you're pulling the muscle
too far or you're holding it too long.

DISTANCE THIS WEEK _____ WEIGHT _____

"There are no shortcuts to any place worth going."   —BEVERLY SILLS

MONDAY, APRIL 7   98

_____

_____

_____

WHERE & WHEN _____ DISTANCE _____

COMMENTS _____

_____

TUESDAY, APRIL 8   99

_____

_____

_____

WHERE & WHEN _____ DISTANCE _____

COMMENTS _____

_____

WEDNESDAY, APRIL 9   100

_____

_____

_____

WHERE & WHEN _____ DISTANCE _____

COMMENTS _____

_____

THURSDAY, APRIL 10   101

_____

_____

_____

WHERE & WHEN _____ DISTANCE _____

COMMENTS _____

_____

FRIDAY, APRIL 11   102

_____

_____

_____

WHERE & WHEN _____ DISTANCE _____

COMMENTS _____

_____

SATURDAY, APRIL 12 103

WHERE & WHEN _____ DISTANCE _____

COMMENTS _____

SUNDAY, APRIL 13 104

WHERE & WHEN _____ DISTANCE _____

COMMENTS _____

"Each one of us has a fire in our heart for something. It's our goal in life to find it and to keep it lit."
—MARY LOU RETTON, 1984 OLYMPIC GOLD-MEDAL WINNER FOR WOMEN'S GYMNASTICS

MONDAY, APRIL 14   105

WHERE & WHEN _____ DISTANCE _____
COMMENTS _____

TUESDAY, APRIL 15   106

WHERE & WHEN _____ DISTANCE _____
COMMENTS _____

WEDNESDAY, APRIL 16   107

WHERE & WHEN _____ DISTANCE _____
COMMENTS _____

THURSDAY, APRIL 17   108

WHERE & WHEN _____ DISTANCE _____
COMMENTS _____

FRIDAY, APRIL 18   109

WHERE & WHEN _____ DISTANCE _____
COMMENTS _____

SATURDAY, APRIL 19 110

_____
_____
_____
_____

WHERE & WHEN _____ DISTANCE _____
COMMENTS _____
_____

SUNDAY, APRIL 20 111

_____
_____
_____
_____

WHERE & WHEN _____ DISTANCE _____
COMMENTS _____
_____

When your schedule is packed, run as early as you can.
Otherwise, your workout will get pushed aside.

DISTANCE THIS WEEK_____ WEIGHT_____

"Our running shoes are really erasers. Every step erases a memory of a past failure. Every mile brings us closer to a clean slate."
—JOHN "THE PENGUIN" BINGHAM, *RUNNER'S WORLD* COLUMNIST

MONDAY, APRIL 21   112

WHERE & WHEN _____ DISTANCE _____
COMMENTS _____

TUESDAY, APRIL 22   113

WHERE & WHEN _____ DISTANCE _____
COMMENTS _____

WEDNESDAY, APRIL 23   114

WHERE & WHEN _____ DISTANCE _____
COMMENTS _____

THURSDAY, APRIL 24   115

WHERE & WHEN _____ DISTANCE _____
COMMENTS _____

FRIDAY, APRIL 25   116

WHERE & WHEN _____ DISTANCE _____
COMMENTS _____

SATURDAY, APRIL 26

WHERE & WHEN _____ DISTANCE _____

COMMENTS _____

SUNDAY, APRIL 27

WHERE & WHEN _____ DISTANCE _____

COMMENTS _____

DISTANCE THIS WEEK _____ WEIGHT _____

MAY

S	M	T	W	T	F	S
				1	2	3
4	5	6	7	8	9	10
11 MOTHER'S DAY	12	13	14	15	16	17
18	19 VICTORIA DAY (CANADA)	20	21	22	23	24
25	26 MEMORIAL DAY	27	28	29	30	31

May: Tunes

Those little white earbuds now adorning athletes everywhere provide an unlikely philosophical flash point. Some runners go nuts at the sight of them, believing Madonna or Mozart intrudes on what should be a single-minded effort and a silent connection with nature: to them, God did not intend for people to run with iPods. To the folks with the earbuds, though, tunes quite simply give them a better workout.

Chalk one up for tunes. A song with a fast tempo early in your run raises your respiratory and heart rates, gently priming you for the hard part of a workout. Music has been proven to extend endurance, though it's not clear why. One theory maintains that it diverts your attention from pain and fatigue, a technique called "dissociation," which distance runners have long employed, with or without music. Another theory suggests that rhythm and melody release dopamine, endorphins, adrenaline, and even steroids into the bloodstream.

The science is fuzzy. Though studies about the effects of music on running extend back to the 1950s, much of the research has been shoddy, even silly. Neuroscience has kicked up the best information we have, however limited. Music stimulates the auditory region of the cerebral cortex—the temporal lobe—which is intimately linked to the limbic system, our body's command center for emotions. Indeed, most runners will tell you they bring music to their workouts not for any performance advantage, but because it makes them happy.

Music and movement have clearly evolved together. After all, dance is integral to most every culture across human history. The next time you can't fall asleep at night, contemplate this: why do human beings dance? For runners, the practical question is whether music moves you faster down the merry path. Science says no. So does the anecdotal evidence. You won't find little white earbuds on any marathon champion. They don't show up at collegiate track-and-field events or at the Olympics. Many coaches won't stand for them in daily workouts.

Serious competition, it seems, requires unwavering focus and vigilance over the myriad subtle signals our bodies send us. Music distracts us from this great business. Even many noncompetitive runners use their workouts as a meditation, a chance to shut out all stimuli unconnected to the task at hand—putting one foot in front of the other, as the Zen master would prescribe. Few of us live so completely in the moment as when we run. It's no surprise that answers to some of the most difficult problems we face arrive soon after a workout has cleared the mind.

Yet even those who are loath to run with music players find that tunes have a place in their workouts—and in competition. A subdued melody right before a race can soothe starting-line jitters. Many runners discover that once they've found their pace, they begin piping a tune through their thoughts, even though it's drawn from memory, not from an iPod. Arguably, it's not music at all. Who cares? Running is private. You can enjoy music any way you like.

"Our society today has become so quick-fix oriented that nobody wants to work over a long period of time for one goal."
—TERRY STANLEY, WINNER OF TWO PRESQUE ISLE MARATHONS, 28 YEARS APART

MONDAY, APRIL 28   119

WHERE & WHEN _____ DISTANCE _____
COMMENTS _____

TUESDAY, APRIL 29   120

WHERE & WHEN _____ DISTANCE _____
COMMENTS _____

WEDNESDAY, APRIL 30   121

WHERE & WHEN _____ DISTANCE _____
COMMENTS _____

THURSDAY, MAY 1   122

WHERE & WHEN _____ DISTANCE _____
COMMENTS _____

FRIDAY, MAY 2   123

WHERE & WHEN _____ DISTANCE _____
COMMENTS _____

WHERE & WHEN _____ DISTANCE _____
COMMENTS _____

WHERE & WHEN _____ DISTANCE _____
COMMENTS _____

Periodically, train by time, not by distance. This lets you take
your workout anywhere, without getting penalized for
wind or hills.

"Workouts are like brushing my teeth; I don't think about them, I just do them. The decision has already been made."

—PATTI SUE PLUMER, U.S. OLYMPIAN

MONDAY, MAY 5   126

WHERE & WHEN _____ DISTANCE _____

COMMENTS _____

TUESDAY, MAY 6   127

WHERE & WHEN _____ DISTANCE _____

COMMENTS _____

WEDNESDAY, MAY 7   128

WHERE & WHEN _____ DISTANCE _____

COMMENTS _____

THURSDAY, MAY 8   129

WHERE & WHEN _____ DISTANCE _____

COMMENTS _____

FRIDAY, MAY 9   130

WHERE & WHEN _____ DISTANCE _____

COMMENTS _____

SATURDAY, MAY 10

WHERE & WHEN _____ DISTANCE _____
COMMENTS _____

SUNDAY, MAY 11

WHERE & WHEN _____ DISTANCE _____
COMMENTS _____

DISTANCE THIS WEEK _____ WEIGHT _____

"Heartbreak Hill felt like a lovely summer day . . . and then you get hit over the head with a hammer." —WILL FERRELL, ACTOR

MONDAY, MAY 12   133

WHERE & WHEN _____ DISTANCE _____
COMMENTS _____

TUESDAY, MAY 13   134

WHERE & WHEN _____ DISTANCE _____
COMMENTS _____

WEDNESDAY, MAY 14   135

WHERE & WHEN _____ DISTANCE _____
COMMENTS _____

THURSDAY, MAY 15   136

WHERE & WHEN _____ DISTANCE _____
COMMENTS _____

FRIDAY, MAY 16   137

WHERE & WHEN _____ DISTANCE _____
COMMENTS _____

SATURDAY, MAY 17

WHERE & WHEN ———————————————— DISTANCE ————

COMMENTS ————————————————————————

SUNDAY, MAY 18

139

WHERE & WHEN ———————————————— DISTANCE ————

COMMENTS ————————————————————————

Fish oil and nuts relieve joint pain and keep your body's
hinges functioning through the years.

"The gun goes off and everything changes . . . the world changes . . . and nothing else really matters." —PATTI SUE PLUMER, U.S. OLYMPIAN

MONDAY, MAY 19   140

WHERE & WHEN _____ DISTANCE _____
COMMENTS _____

TUESDAY, MAY 20   141

WHERE & WHEN _____ DISTANCE _____
COMMENTS _____

WEDNESDAY, MAY 21   142

WHERE & WHEN _____ DISTANCE _____
COMMENTS _____

THURSDAY, MAY 22   143

WHERE & WHEN _____ DISTANCE _____
COMMENTS _____

FRIDAY, MAY 23   144

WHERE & WHEN _____ DISTANCE _____
COMMENTS _____

WHERE & WHEN ⎯⎯⎯⎯⎯⎯⎯⎯⎯⎯⎯⎯⎯⎯⎯⎯ DISTANCE ⎯⎯⎯⎯⎯
COMMENTS ⎯⎯⎯⎯⎯⎯⎯⎯⎯⎯⎯⎯⎯⎯⎯⎯⎯⎯⎯⎯⎯⎯⎯⎯⎯⎯⎯⎯

WHERE & WHEN ⎯⎯⎯⎯⎯⎯⎯⎯⎯⎯⎯⎯⎯⎯⎯⎯ DISTANCE ⎯⎯⎯⎯⎯
COMMENTS ⎯⎯⎯⎯⎯⎯⎯⎯⎯⎯⎯⎯⎯⎯⎯⎯⎯⎯⎯⎯⎯⎯⎯⎯⎯⎯⎯⎯

DISTANCE THIS WEEK ⎯⎯⎯⎯⎯⎯⎯⎯⎯⎯⎯ WEIGHT ⎯⎯⎯⎯⎯

JUNE

S	M	T	W	T	F	S
1	2	3	4	5	6	7
8	9	10	11	12	13	14
15 FATHER'S DAY	16	17	18	19	20	21
22	23	24	25	26	27	28
29	30					

June: Miracles

Do you smell fraud in a training program that promises to prepare any runner for a marathon in 12 weeks' time by running only three days a week? As with Internet college degrees or miracle hair restoration, you should examine the fine print before you hand over your money.

To be fair, there's great efficacy in exchanging miles for intensity in your workouts. Coaches everywhere are finding that they get more from their runners—in both speed and endurance—by dialing back the distance in favor of interval sets, tempo runs, and cross training. This is not a fad. Lowering weekly mileage reduces the risk of injury. It allows for more recovery time, which is how muscle is forged. It also lets you have a life beyond running.

The trick to low-mileage workouts is to recognize when you're slipping into folly, which isn't always readily apparent. The two best-tested programs for the less-is-more path to a marathon focus on the weekly long run, gradually adding one mile, then two, per week until you're running 17 miles or more. Former Olympian Jeff Galloway trains his marathoners with thrice-weekly workouts, dedicating two of them to intervals and tempo runs—methodical, graduated sets that require stopwatches and fierce dedication. He emphasizes lots of one-minute walk breaks. Galloway doesn't promise miracles (it's a six-month program for beginners), but over the years, his clinics have helped thousands of people cross the finish line for the first time. He's helped many more shave minutes off their personal-best marathon times.

The other proven type of low-mileage program augments running workouts with aerobic cross training, typically through non-weight-bearing exercises such as swimming, bicycling, using elliptical trainers, and the like. The best of these comes from Furman University in Greenville, South Carolina. As with Galloway's regimen, the Furman Institute of Running and Scientific Training (FIRST) program features a weekly long run, a shorter workout of tempo runs, and a day of interval training. It also adds two days of cross training. While the FIRST program demands more of your week for workouts, it promises to put you on the starting line of a marathon in four months flat.

Does this invite disaster? Before embarking on the FIRST program, you should be comfortable running at least eight miles, a prerequisite that requires interpretation—the "comfortable" part, that is. What we know about injury is that the number of years you've been running is a better indication of your stamina than the number of miles you run each week. What we know about disappointment is that the marathon is an unfathomably long distance to ramp up to quickly. Crash programs won't get you there.

The genius of both the Galloway and the FIRST programs lies in how they inform your workouts, not your goals. It is undeniably true that distance runners can get more for less. Perhaps you can even run a marathon after four months of dedicated effort. A smarter bet: let your legs tell you when it's time for a marathon.

"Dream barriers look very high until someone climbs them. Then they are not barriers anymore."

—LASSE VIRÉN, FOUR-TIME OLYMPIC GOLD-MEDAL WINNER

MONDAY, MAY 26   147

WHERE & WHEN _____ DISTANCE _____
COMMENTS _____

TUESDAY, MAY 27   148

WHERE & WHEN _____ DISTANCE _____
COMMENTS _____

WEDNESDAY, MAY 28   149

WHERE & WHEN _____ DISTANCE _____
COMMENTS _____

THURSDAY, MAY 29   150

WHERE & WHEN _____ DISTANCE _____
COMMENTS _____

FRIDAY, MAY 30   151

WHERE & WHEN _____ DISTANCE _____
COMMENTS _____

WHERE & WHEN _____ DISTANCE _____
COMMENTS _____

WHERE & WHEN _____ DISTANCE _____
COMMENTS _____

Poor posture makes poor running form. See, your mother
was right all along.

DISTANCE THIS WEEK _____ WEIGHT_____

"Ask yourself, Can I give more? The answer is usually yes."
—PAUL TERGAT, MARATHON WORLD-RECORD HOLDER (2:04:55)

MONDAY, JUNE 2   154

WHERE & WHEN _____ DISTANCE _____
COMMENTS _____

TUESDAY, JUNE 3   155

WHERE & WHEN _____ DISTANCE _____
COMMENTS _____

WEDNESDAY, JUNE 4   156

WHERE & WHEN _____ DISTANCE _____
COMMENTS _____

THURSDAY, JUNE 5   157

WHERE & WHEN _____ DISTANCE _____
COMMENTS _____

FRIDAY, JUNE 6   158

WHERE & WHEN _____ DISTANCE _____
COMMENTS _____

SATURDAY, JUNE 7

WHERE & WHEN _____ DISTANCE _____

COMMENTS _____

SUNDAY, JUNE 8

WHERE & WHEN _____ DISTANCE _____

COMMENTS _____

DISTANCE THIS WEEK _____ WEIGHT _____

"When I perform, I can tell the days I haven't run. The clarity in my voice isn't the same."

—JO DEE MESSINA, GRAMMY-NOMINATED COUNTRY MUSIC SINGER

MONDAY, JUNE 9   161

WHERE & WHEN _____ DISTANCE _____
COMMENTS _____

TUESDAY, JUNE 10   162

WHERE & WHEN _____ DISTANCE _____
COMMENTS _____

WEDNESDAY, JUNE 11   163

WHERE & WHEN _____ DISTANCE _____
COMMENTS _____

THURSDAY, JUNE 12   164

WHERE & WHEN _____ DISTANCE _____
COMMENTS _____

FRIDAY, JUNE 13   165

WHERE & WHEN _____ DISTANCE _____
COMMENTS _____

SATURDAY, JUNE 14

WHERE & WHEN _____ DISTANCE _____

COMMENTS _____

SUNDAY, JUNE 15

WHERE & WHEN _____ DISTANCE _____

COMMENTS _____

Running before you're 40 reduces joint and muscle pain by
up to 25 percent in later years, especially after the age of 62.

DISTANCE THIS WEEK _____ WEIGHT _____

"Goals are about the lightest thing you have to travel with."

—JOSH RITTER, SINGER-SONGWRITER

MONDAY, JUNE 16   168

WHERE & WHEN _____ DISTANCE _____
COMMENTS _____

TUESDAY, JUNE 17   169

WHERE & WHEN _____ DISTANCE _____
COMMENTS _____

WEDNESDAY, JUNE 18   170

WHERE & WHEN _____ DISTANCE _____
COMMENTS _____

THURSDAY, JUNE 19   171

WHERE & WHEN _____ DISTANCE _____
COMMENTS _____

FRIDAY, JUNE 20   172

WHERE & WHEN _____ DISTANCE _____
COMMENTS _____

WHERE & WHEN _____ DISTANCE _____

COMMENTS _____

WHERE & WHEN _____ DISTANCE _____

COMMENTS _____

If you're prone to Achilles tendonitis, calf-muscle injuries, or plantar fasciitis (severe pain in the heel, especially when you put weight on it upon getting out of bed), slow your pace on the treadmill—and don't do inclines.

DISTANCE THIS WEEK _____ WEIGHT _____

"When runners complain of overuse injuries, it's a safe bet they're running on roads."

—ADAM CHASE, COAUTHOR OF *THE ULTIMATE GUIDE TO TRAIL RUNNING*

MONDAY, JUNE 23   175

WHERE & WHEN _____ DISTANCE _____

COMMENTS _____

TUESDAY, JUNE 24   176

WHERE & WHEN _____ DISTANCE _____

COMMENTS _____

WEDNESDAY, JUNE 25   177

WHERE & WHEN _____ DISTANCE _____

COMMENTS _____

THURSDAY, JUNE 26   178

WHERE & WHEN _____ DISTANCE _____

COMMENTS _____

FRIDAY, JUNE 27   179

WHERE & WHEN _____ DISTANCE _____

COMMENTS _____

SATURDAY, JUNE 28

180

WHERE & WHEN —————————————————— DISTANCE ———————
COMMENTS ——————————————————————————————————

SUNDAY, JUNE 29

181

WHERE & WHEN —————————————————— DISTANCE ———————
COMMENTS ——————————————————————————————————

Tapering your workouts before an event increases your body's
oxygen uptake and decreases muscular fatigue. It's also likely
to put you in a better mood.

JULY

S	M	T	W	T	F	S
		1 CANADA DAY	2	3	4 INDEPENDENCE DAY	5
6	7	8	9	10	11	12
13	14	15	16	17	18	19
20	21	22	23	24	25	26
27	28	29	30	31		

July: Mortals

You run for your life. Whether you ultimately chase trophies, slender thighs, tranquillity, or vindication, the benefits of running cascade across every aspect of your health, including your mental equilibrium. Even so, you probably know that more running doesn't yield still more robust health. In fact, most evidence suggests that the benefits peak with moderate amounts of exercise. To most runners, this is counterintuitive. Nothing makes us feel more alive than the vigor and satisfaction that come from hard training.

Unfortunately, you tempt fate by trusting your intuition on matters of health. You can't outrun your genes, for example. If you have a family history of stroke or heart disease, your training program should proceed under the watchful eye of a physician, especially if you're male and over 35. Even if you've been running hard for decades, cardiovascular problems can erupt suddenly and without warning. The American Heart Association provides guidelines for athletes with a family history of heart disease. Periodically, you should ask your doctor about a cardiogram and possibly a treadmill test.

Nor can you outrun years of debauchery, though a good training program can halt physical decline as if you'd lassoed it. This is deceptive. Running makes you look younger and feel better, which makes it easy to entertain the delusion that hard training erases Twinkies and cigarettes and long afternoons with the TV remote in your hand. The truth is that smoking, cholesterol, obesity, and even stress wreak cumulative damage. Great efforts have been made to prove that running reverses these assaults. Alas, the best evidence we have shows otherwise.

Almost as depressing is the mistaken hope that you can run back into the embrace of your youth. Those who begin running in their later years don't feel compelled to recapture bygone glories. Everyone else trains harder to retain yesteryear's abilities. As you age, you must eventually change your goals, change your measures of achievement. Face up to hard limits. It's a psychological leap that usually brings relief and sacrifices little in the satisfaction you get from running. The secret lies in mustering the humility to make that leap before a moment of reckoning confronts you.

You also have to acknowledge the constants of injury and illness. In the big picture of health, a good training program wards off these problems and helps you recover quickly when they sneak past your defenses. So why do runners invariably feel surprised and furious when suddenly wounded? At some unconscious level, we talk ourselves into believing that training makes us immortal. It's a perilous kind of thinking, a natural result of the innocent fulfillment we get from running. It's why we rush recovery, often with disastrous results.

It's also why we deny we're sick or injured in the first place. In fact, a good training program feeds all manner of dangerous thinking. It's ironic: running makes us feel more alive than ever. At the very least, it should allow us to be human.

"Mind is everything: muscle—pieces of rubber. All that I am, I am because of my mind." —PAAVO NURMI, WINNER OF 12 OLYMPIC MEDALS

MONDAY, JUNE 30   182

WHERE & WHEN _____ DISTANCE _____
COMMENTS _____

TUESDAY, JULY 1   183

WHERE & WHEN _____ DISTANCE _____
COMMENTS _____

WEDNESDAY, JULY 2   184

WHERE & WHEN _____ DISTANCE _____
COMMENTS _____

THURSDAY, JULY 3   185

WHERE & WHEN _____ DISTANCE _____
COMMENTS _____

FRIDAY, JULY 4   186

WHERE & WHEN _____ DISTANCE _____
COMMENTS _____

SATURDAY, JULY 5

WHERE & WHEN ⎯⎯⎯⎯⎯⎯⎯⎯⎯⎯⎯⎯⎯ DISTANCE ⎯⎯⎯⎯
COMMENTS ⎯⎯⎯⎯⎯⎯⎯⎯⎯⎯⎯⎯⎯⎯⎯⎯⎯⎯⎯⎯

SUNDAY, JULY 6

WHERE & WHEN ⎯⎯⎯⎯⎯⎯⎯⎯⎯⎯⎯⎯⎯ DISTANCE ⎯⎯⎯⎯
COMMENTS ⎯⎯⎯⎯⎯⎯⎯⎯⎯⎯⎯⎯⎯⎯⎯⎯⎯⎯⎯⎯

Contrary to popular myth, women tend to recover from hard
workouts more quickly than men do.

DISTANCE THIS WEEK⎯⎯⎯⎯⎯⎯⎯⎯⎯⎯ WEIGHT⎯⎯⎯⎯⎯

"I tell our runners to divide the race into thirds. Run the first part with your head, the middle part with your personality, and the last part with your heart." —MIKE FANELLI, FORMER COACH FOR THE SAN FRANCISCO IMPALAS

MONDAY, JULY 7 189

WHERE & WHEN _____ DISTANCE _____
COMMENTS _____

TUESDAY, JULY 8 190

WHERE & WHEN _____ DISTANCE _____
COMMENTS _____

WEDNESDAY, JULY 9 191

WHERE & WHEN _____ DISTANCE _____
COMMENTS _____

THURSDAY, JULY 10 192

WHERE & WHEN _____ DISTANCE _____
COMMENTS _____

FRIDAY, JULY 11 193

WHERE & WHEN _____ DISTANCE _____
COMMENTS _____

WHERE & WHEN _____ DISTANCE _____
COMMENTS _____

WHERE & WHEN _____ DISTANCE _____
COMMENTS _____

Most freeze-dried fruits pack as much nutritional value—
including antioxidants—as their fresh counterparts.

"Perseverance is not a long race; it is many short races, one after another."
—WALTER ELLIOTT

MONDAY, JULY 14   196

WHERE & WHEN _____ DISTANCE _____
COMMENTS _____

TUESDAY, JULY 15   197

WHERE & WHEN _____ DISTANCE _____
COMMENTS _____

WEDNESDAY, JULY 16   198

WHERE & WHEN _____ DISTANCE _____
COMMENTS _____

THURSDAY, JULY 17   199

WHERE & WHEN _____ DISTANCE _____
COMMENTS _____

FRIDAY, JULY 18   200

WHERE & WHEN _____ DISTANCE _____
COMMENTS _____

WHERE & WHEN _____ DISTANCE _____
COMMENTS _____

WHERE & WHEN _____ DISTANCE _____
COMMENTS _____

When running in hot weather, make sure you get plenty of
potassium: eat bananas, citrus fruits, dates, raisins,
and potatoes.

DISTANCE THIS WEEK_____ WEIGHT_____

"You can outdistance that which is running after you, but not what is running inside you."
—RWANDAN PROVERB

MONDAY, JULY 21   203

WHERE & WHEN _____ DISTANCE _____
COMMENTS _____

TUESDAY, JULY 22   204

WHERE & WHEN _____ DISTANCE _____
COMMENTS _____

WEDNESDAY, JULY 23   205

WHERE & WHEN _____ DISTANCE _____
COMMENTS _____

THURSDAY, JULY 24   206

WHERE & WHEN _____ DISTANCE _____
COMMENTS _____

FRIDAY, JULY 25   207

WHERE & WHEN _____ DISTANCE _____
COMMENTS _____

SATURDAY, JULY 26

_____

_____

_____

WHERE & WHEN _____ DISTANCE _____

COMMENTS _____

_____

SUNDAY, JULY 27

_____

_____

_____

WHERE & WHEN _____ DISTANCE _____

COMMENTS _____

_____

To avoid injury, start with five intervals, then add only one or two repetitions to each successive workout—and knock off a day (or cross train) between these workouts.

DISTANCE THIS WEEK _____ WEIGHT _____

AUGUST

S	M	T	W	T	F	S
					1	2
3	4	5	6	7	8	9
10	11	12	13	14	15	16
17	18	19	20	21	22	23
24	25	26	27	28	29	30
31						

August: Sole

Lose the shoes and watch your performance fly? Barefoot runners tread the quirky fringe of serious fitness. The very idea of taking your regular run with naked heels and toe pads pounding into pavement probably sends a shudder through your gut. And yet barefooters are beginning to find legitimacy, even vindication.

South African Zola Budd twice broke world records in the women's 5000 meters, both times without wearing shoes. Ethiopian Abebe Bikila won two consecutive Olympic marathons unshod. And Bassirima Soro, an Ivory Coast native, won his fifth Tucson Marathon by shedding his shoes at mile 14. Is there something about the African continent that gives human feet titanium soles . . . and also wings?

More likely, we Westerners coddle our feet like babies who refuse to grow strong. In fact, barefoot advocates suggest that we're begging for injury. Good running shoes, with their rigid soles and cushioned inserts, allow feet to become lazy. Worse, they change our natural running form so that shins, ankles, back muscles, and hips bear awkward loads with each step. One Canadian study has shown that heavily cushioned shoes are more likely to provoke injury than simpler designs. There's growing evidence that motion-control shoes do more harm than good. And there's little question that shoes of any kind squander energy in the same way that soft, underinflated tires result in poor gas mileage for your car.

Scientific research on barefoot running is scant. Its popularity has been advanced by skin-to-the-pavement evangelists, their growing ranks apparent at any marathon or 10K event. The trend hasn't been lost on shoemakers, at least two of which now offer models that mimic the sensation of running barefoot without the broken glass, gravel, and grime. Indeed, minimalist footwear is quickly turning into a sensation. Those not quite willing to bare all are turning to ballet slippers, boat shoes, and other thin-soled apparel that provides a minimum of protection while letting the foot connect with the ground in as natural a way as possible.

Podiatrists are horrified by this whole business. They'll tell you that barefoot running is a no-no for anyone with diabetes since simple foot wounds can lead to serious complications. Impact injuries to joints and connective tissue will be exaggerated when you run barefoot. Scrapes and puncture wounds may seem tolerably painful, but it's important to remember that streets are full of bacteria, germs, and fungi. So are trails that meander through glorious, pristine forests.

Are you still game? Many converts to barefoot running suffered intractable pains in their shoes that years of advice failed to solve. But even the most ardent proponents will tell you to begin slowly. Grass and indoor tracks are the best places to initiate your naked feet. Give them plenty of time to heal between workouts. Advance to clean sidewalks. All of these workouts should be relatively short augmentations of your regular training program. Seek to learn from them. Who knows? If the experience is good, you may start rethinking your running shorts, too.

"The difference between a jogger and a runner is an entry form."

—GEORGE SHEEHAN

MONDAY, JULY 28   210

WHERE & WHEN _____ DISTANCE _____
COMMENTS _____

TUESDAY, JULY 29   211

WHERE & WHEN _____ DISTANCE _____
COMMENTS _____

WEDNESDAY, JULY 30   212

WHERE & WHEN _____ DISTANCE _____
COMMENTS _____

THURSDAY, JULY 31   213

WHERE & WHEN _____ DISTANCE _____
COMMENTS _____

FRIDAY, AUGUST 1   214

WHERE & WHEN _____ DISTANCE _____
COMMENTS _____

SATURDAY, AUGUST 2

WHERE & WHEN _____ DISTANCE _____
COMMENTS _____

SUNDAY, AUGUST 3

WHERE & WHEN _____ DISTANCE _____
COMMENTS _____

"Some days you'll run and no matter how hard you think you're going, you'll never be quick. Then there are those days when you're lightning. No reason why." —DAN WHELDON, INDIANAPOLIS 500 CHAMPION

MONDAY, AUGUST 4　　　　　　　　　217

WHERE & WHEN _____ DISTANCE _____
COMMENTS _____

TUESDAY, AUGUST 5　　　　　　　　　218

WHERE & WHEN _____ DISTANCE _____
COMMENTS _____

WEDNESDAY, AUGUST 6　　　　　　　　219

WHERE & WHEN _____ DISTANCE _____
COMMENTS _____

THURSDAY, AUGUST 7　　　　　　　　220

WHERE & WHEN _____ DISTANCE _____
COMMENTS _____

FRIDAY, AUGUST 8　　　　　　　　　221

WHERE & WHEN _____ DISTANCE _____
COMMENTS _____

WHERE & WHEN _____ DISTANCE _____

COMMENTS _____

WHERE & WHEN _____ DISTANCE _____

COMMENTS _____

Losing even a few pounds if you're overweight can
dramatically improve your sex life.

DISTANCE THIS WEEK _____ WEIGHT _____

"I started doing triathlons because the training is so varied. With three sports . . . there isn't much chance of getting bored."
—HEATHER FUHR, FIVE-TIME LAKE PLACID IRONMAN CHAMPION

MONDAY, AUGUST 11   224

WHERE & WHEN _____ DISTANCE _____
COMMENTS _____

TUESDAY, AUGUST 12   225

WHERE & WHEN _____ DISTANCE _____
COMMENTS _____

WEDNESDAY, AUGUST 13   226

WHERE & WHEN _____ DISTANCE _____
COMMENTS _____

THURSDAY, AUGUST 14   227

WHERE & WHEN _____ DISTANCE _____
COMMENTS _____

FRIDAY, AUGUST 15   228

WHERE & WHEN _____ DISTANCE _____
COMMENTS _____

WHERE & WHEN _____ DISTANCE _____
COMMENTS _____

WHERE & WHEN _____ DISTANCE _____
COMMENTS _____

Lacing your shoes backward—tying them at the toes—can
relieve pressure on your peroneal nerve, which is the source
of much foot and ankle pain.

DISTANCE THIS WEEK _____ WEIGHT _____

"The most important aspect of training is consistency."
—JENNIFER TOOMEY, TWO-TIME U.S. INDOOR 1500-METER CHAMPION

MONDAY, AUGUST 18   231

WHERE & WHEN _____ DISTANCE _____
COMMENTS _____

TUESDAY, AUGUST 19   232

WHERE & WHEN _____ DISTANCE _____
COMMENTS _____

WEDNESDAY, AUGUST 20   233

WHERE & WHEN _____ DISTANCE _____
COMMENTS _____

THURSDAY, AUGUST 21   234

WHERE & WHEN _____ DISTANCE _____
COMMENTS _____

FRIDAY, AUGUST 22   235

WHERE & WHEN _____ DISTANCE _____
COMMENTS _____

SATURDAY, AUGUST 23

WHERE & WHEN _____ DISTANCE _____

COMMENTS _____

SUNDAY, AUGUST 24

WHERE & WHEN _____ DISTANCE _____

COMMENTS _____

The most common culprits of injury are high mileage,
a history of injury, and a lack of recovery time
between workouts.

DISTANCE THIS WEEK_____ WEIGHT_____

"What's the greatest running gadget? Ice. As I get older, it's become a cure for everything." —TATE DONOVAN, ACTOR

MONDAY, AUGUST 25 238

WHERE & WHEN _____ DISTANCE _____
COMMENTS _____

TUESDAY, AUGUST 26 239

WHERE & WHEN _____ DISTANCE _____
COMMENTS _____

WEDNESDAY, AUGUST 27 240

WHERE & WHEN _____ DISTANCE _____
COMMENTS _____

THURSDAY, AUGUST 28 241

WHERE & WHEN _____ DISTANCE _____
COMMENTS _____

FRIDAY, AUGUST 29 242

WHERE & WHEN _____ DISTANCE _____
COMMENTS _____

WHERE & WHEN _____ DISTANCE _____

COMMENTS _____

SUNDAY, AUGUST 31

244

WHERE & WHEN _____ DISTANCE _____

COMMENTS _____

DISTANCE THIS WEEK _____ WEIGHT _____

SEPTEMBER

S	M	T	W	T	F	S
		1 LABOR DAY	2	3	4	5	6
7	8	9	10	11	12	13
14	15	16	17	18	19	20
21	22	23	24	25	26	27
28	29	30 ROSH HASHANAH				

September: Racer

You can resist the temptation of joining a religious cult or a career in knocking over liquor stores—at least you tell yourself so. But a racing registration form is such a guileless seduction, such a win-win bargain. Regardless of the event, you can aim for any number of goals in a single contest, all of them determined by your own fevered imagination. Besides, if it turns out that you don't like racing, you can simply walk away, lesson learned.

This is essentially what Napoléon thought about Russia. To be sure, there's a lot to gain from competition, especially from the focus and organization it brings to your training. The calendar imposes a date; all effort is directed toward the crack of the starting gun. Gone are the flatliner workouts you plod through from some dutiful goal of fitness or weight loss. Racing puts a snap in your step. It thrills the heart by forcing you to look at tangible improvement.

And then what? The workouts to worry about aren't those that lead up to a race, but those that follow. Racing enthusiasm usually collapses the day after an event, especially after a long-distance race such as a marathon. This is where many running programs perish. Experienced racers fill their calendars with multiple events, knowing that many of these will be scratched, but also knowing that any single race is not a crusade; multiple events make disappointments easier to take. They also keep training programs alive by spreading goals across the year, allowing them to evolve. First-timers should plan to train down to very easy workouts for the two weeks following a race, until everything heals. But it's important to begin building back toward a goal soon afterward.

Should that goal be another race? The question may not provoke an identity crisis, but it invites healthy reflection. Each year, millions of runners become hooked on competition after exactly one race, bringing with them no more ambition than simply to cross the finish line again and again. The tribal energy of racing—the shared enthusiasm—supplies all the motivation these runners need to keep their training programs delivering results. Racing throws doors open. It makes public a very private part of who you are.

Trouble lies where more ambitious goals are at stake. Obviously, you can't set a personal record with each event; you will ultimately run into the wall of your own abilities. You must also confront age. The marvelous fact about running is that there are competitive events for every age and ability imaginable. Still, the initial thrills of crowds, concentrated effort, and successive victories eventually subside. Too often these take the love of running with them. You need only look at the high school track star who's morphed into a middle-aged pear to see the dangers of loving competition too much.

The secret to racing is in keeping the love of training alive. As your goals and expectations change, your daily workouts are the constant that will sustain you even after humiliating defeats, after you've had to face cruel truths about your abilities. In fact, the real secret about racing is that training is as sweet as any victory.

"Road racing is rock 'n' roll; track is Carnegie Hall."
—MARTY LIQUORI, MUSICIAN AND ONETIME RECORD HOLDER
FOR THE AMERICAN MEN'S 2K, 5K, AND 2 MILES

MONDAY, SEPTEMBER 1   245

WHERE & WHEN _____ DISTANCE _____
COMMENTS _____

TUESDAY, SEPTEMBER 2   246

WHERE & WHEN _____ DISTANCE _____
COMMENTS _____

WEDNESDAY, SEPTEMBER 3   247

WHERE & WHEN _____ DISTANCE _____
COMMENTS _____

THURSDAY, SEPTEMBER 4   248

WHERE & WHEN _____ DISTANCE _____
COMMENTS _____

FRIDAY, SEPTEMBER 5   249

WHERE & WHEN _____ DISTANCE _____
COMMENTS _____

SATURDAY, SEPTEMBER 6

WHERE & WHEN _____ DISTANCE _____
COMMENTS _____

SUNDAY, SEPTEMBER 7

251

WHERE & WHEN _____ DISTANCE _____
COMMENTS _____

Losing your motivation? Switch to trail running once a week,
get a running partner, or add new songs to your iPod.

DISTANCE THIS WEEK _____ WEIGHT _____

"The memory of fallen soldiers and their families kept me going."
——RAY GOMEZ, SPFC, AFTER COMPLETING A 6-DAY,
156-MILE RUN THROUGH THE SAHARA

MONDAY, SEPTEMBER 8   252

WHERE & WHEN _____ DISTANCE _____
COMMENTS _____

TUESDAY, SEPTEMBER 9   253

WHERE & WHEN _____ DISTANCE _____
COMMENTS _____

WEDNESDAY, SEPTEMBER 10   254

WHERE & WHEN _____ DISTANCE _____
COMMENTS _____

THURSDAY, SEPTEMBER 11   255

WHERE & WHEN _____ DISTANCE _____
COMMENTS _____

FRIDAY, SEPTEMBER 12   256

WHERE & WHEN _____ DISTANCE _____
COMMENTS _____

WHERE & WHEN _____ DISTANCE _____

COMMENTS _____

WHERE & WHEN _____ DISTANCE _____

COMMENTS _____

Exercise can help strengthen knee cartilage and improve joint function in people who suffer knee osteoarthritis.

"To me, life is in the struggle. I never feel more alive than when I'm struggling." ——DEAN KARNAZES, AUTHOR OF *ULTRAMARATHON MAN*

MONDAY, SEPTEMBER 15 259

WHERE & WHEN _____ DISTANCE _____
COMMENTS _____

TUESDAY, SEPTEMBER 16 260

WHERE & WHEN _____ DISTANCE _____
COMMENTS _____

WEDNESDAY, SEPTEMBER 17 261

WHERE & WHEN _____ DISTANCE _____
COMMENTS _____

THURSDAY, SEPTEMBER 18 262

WHERE & WHEN _____ DISTANCE _____
COMMENTS _____

FRIDAY, SEPTEMBER 19 263

WHERE & WHEN _____ DISTANCE _____
COMMENTS _____

SATURDAY, SEPTEMBER 20

WHERE & WHEN _____ DISTANCE _____
COMMENTS _____

SUNDAY, SEPTEMBER 21

WHERE & WHEN _____ DISTANCE _____
COMMENTS _____

DISTANCE THIS WEEK _____ WEIGHT _____

"I'm usually in the top 5 percent of my age category. Once you're over 50, there aren't many Kenyans and Ethiopians in your group."
—RICHARD OPSAHL, 73, ON HIS 24TH NEW YORK CITY MARATHON

MONDAY, SEPTEMBER 22   266

WHERE & WHEN _____ DISTANCE _____
COMMENTS _____

TUESDAY, SEPTEMBER 23   267

WHERE & WHEN _____ DISTANCE _____
COMMENTS _____

WEDNESDAY, SEPTEMBER 24   268

WHERE & WHEN _____ DISTANCE _____
COMMENTS _____

THURSDAY, SEPTEMBER 25   269

WHERE & WHEN _____ DISTANCE _____
COMMENTS _____

FRIDAY, SEPTEMBER 26   270

WHERE & WHEN _____ DISTANCE _____
COMMENTS _____

WHERE & WHEN _____ DISTANCE _____
COMMENTS _____

WHERE & WHEN _____ DISTANCE _____
COMMENTS _____

If it *can* chafe, it *will* chafe—on any distance over eight miles.
At least you should plan this way. Dress and lubricate
accordingly.

OCTOBER

S	M	T	W	T	F	S
			1	2	3	4
5	6	7	8	9 YOM KIPPUR	10	11
12	13 COLUMBUS DAY	14	15	16	17	18
19	20	21	22	23	24 UNITED NATIONS DAY	25
26	27	28	29	30	31 HALLOWEEN	

October: Voices

Olympic track stars talk a lot about working in "the zone," that transcendent mental state in which each footstep proceeds without conscious effort, the mind seemingly still. Run in the zone, and your performance soars. All runners experience it from time to time. Many devote years to building training regimes timed to conjure it on race day.

Yet growing ranks of experts now say *fuggedaboutit.* Mentally speaking, it's better to build the confidence that allows you to fall off your peak performance—even for extended periods—knowing that you can regain it. Without this confidence, you're apt to go spiraling into a full-fledged slump, which often only gets worse the harder you work. While slumps seem to come from nowhere (and runners tend to be downright superstitious about them), they often stem from a lack of mental preparation.

Before you pooh-pooh the role of psychology in running, consider what happens when a loud, mysterious crash in the house wakes you at three in the morning. Instantly, the fog of sleep clears, thanks to adrenaline pumping through your body. Your heart races. And if you're unable to identify the source of the noise after several seconds of logical deduction, your palms will begin to sweat. In other words, rational thoughts have a direct effect on very primitive (autonomic) parts of the nervous system. So it is with runners and their honed, complex motor skills. Like it or not, your thoughts affect your performance.

For most of us, running is so innate, so seemingly ingrained in our muscles, that our thoughts tend to float above the effort. This is where trouble brews. Our heads resonate with interminable voices as we process events—what psychologists call self-talk. There's more chatter than you might imagine, anywhere from 60 to 1,000 words per minute. As fatigue makes itself at home, these voices begin murmuring about failure, often without basis. When familiar competitors shoot ahead of you in a race, you're apt to tell yourself that you've lost your edge, which can set off a fight-or-flight response, releasing adrenaline and narrowing your field of vision. It's a self-defeating response.

There's no way to stop negative thoughts, but you can train yourself to detect their arrival. Sports psychologists teach a technique called thought swapping, which is just a fancy kind of diversion: if you can't quiet the voices in your head, make them change the subject. Visualization is one trick. When negative thoughts arrive, try to evoke images of the course ahead of you: wide bends, grassy descents, or narrow passages where challenges and opportunities lurk. Relaxation techniques, especially deep-breathing exercises, can quell pre-race jitters and other forms of anxiety. Many runners turn to meditation, even prayer.

Will thought swapping let you run in the zone? Not likely, but the best mental training strategies don't attempt to summon magic; they free you from self-doubt. Besides, the voices in your head aren't always negative. Hope, resolve, and victory may be little more than whispers, but pay attention to them.

"Concerts deplete me; running energizes me."
—CARTER BREY, PRINCIPAL CELLIST, NEW YORK PHILHARMONIC

MONDAY, SEPTEMBER 29   273

WHERE & WHEN _____ DISTANCE _____
COMMENTS _____

TUESDAY, SEPTEMBER 30   274

WHERE & WHEN _____ DISTANCE _____
COMMENTS _____

WEDNESDAY, OCTOBER 1   275

WHERE & WHEN _____ DISTANCE _____
COMMENTS _____

THURSDAY, OCTOBER 2   276

WHERE & WHEN _____ DISTANCE _____
COMMENTS _____

FRIDAY, OCTOBER 3   277

WHERE & WHEN _____ DISTANCE _____
COMMENTS _____

WHERE & WHEN _____ DISTANCE _____
COMMENTS _____

WHERE & WHEN _____ DISTANCE _____
COMMENTS _____

Glucosamine and chondroitin, never mind how you
pronounce them, are effective at reducing knee pain and
other osteoarthritis aches.

"Good things come slow—especially in distance running."
—BILL DELLINGER, RUNNING COACH, UNIVERSITY OF OREGON

MONDAY, OCTOBER 6 280

WHERE & WHEN _____ DISTANCE _____
COMMENTS _____

TUESDAY, OCTOBER 7 281

WHERE & WHEN _____ DISTANCE _____
COMMENTS _____

WEDNESDAY, OCTOBER 8 282

WHERE & WHEN _____ DISTANCE _____
COMMENTS _____

THURSDAY, OCTOBER 9 283

WHERE & WHEN _____ DISTANCE _____
COMMENTS _____

FRIDAY, OCTOBER 10 284

WHERE & WHEN _____ DISTANCE _____
COMMENTS _____

WHERE & WHEN _____ DISTANCE _____
COMMENTS _____

WHERE & WHEN _____ DISTANCE _____
COMMENTS _____

DISTANCE THIS WEEK _____ WEIGHT _____

"If the hill has its own name, then it's probably a pretty tough hill."
—MARTY STERN, FIVE-TIME WINNING COACH FOR NCAA MEN'S CROSS-COUNTRY

MONDAY, OCTOBER 13   287

WHERE & WHEN _____ DISTANCE _____
COMMENTS _____

TUESDAY, OCTOBER 14   288

WHERE & WHEN _____ DISTANCE _____
COMMENTS _____

WEDNESDAY, OCTOBER 15   289

WHERE & WHEN _____ DISTANCE _____
COMMENTS _____

THURSDAY, OCTOBER 16   290

WHERE & WHEN _____ DISTANCE _____
COMMENTS _____

FRIDAY, OCTOBER 17   291

WHERE & WHEN _____ DISTANCE _____
COMMENTS _____

WHERE & WHEN _____ DISTANCE _____
COMMENTS _____

SUNDAY, OCTOBER 19   293

WHERE & WHEN _____ DISTANCE _____
COMMENTS _____

In any distance race, lock in to your pace early and resist the
urge to kick it up mid-race. Endurance is tested
in the last 15 percent.

DISTANCE THIS WEEK _____ WEIGHT _____

"It is true that speed kills. In distance running, it kills anyone who does not have it."

—BROOKS JOHNSON, U.S. OLYMPIC COACH FOR WOMEN'S RUNNING

MONDAY, OCTOBER 20   294

WHERE & WHEN _____ DISTANCE _____
COMMENTS _____

TUESDAY, OCTOBER 21   295

WHERE & WHEN _____ DISTANCE _____
COMMENTS _____

WEDNESDAY, OCTOBER 22   296

WHERE & WHEN _____ DISTANCE _____
COMMENTS _____

THURSDAY, OCTOBER 23   297

WHERE & WHEN _____ DISTANCE _____
COMMENTS _____

FRIDAY, OCTOBER 24   298

WHERE & WHEN _____ DISTANCE _____
COMMENTS _____

WHERE & WHEN _____ DISTANCE _____
COMMENTS _____

WHERE & WHEN _____ DISTANCE _____
COMMENTS _____

NOVEMBER

S	M	T	W	T	F	S
						1
2	3	4	5	6	7	8
9	10	11 VETERANS DAY	12	13	14	15
16	17	18	19	20	21	22
23	24	25	26	27 THANKSGIVING DAY	28	29
30						

November: Clowns

Among the childhood pleasures we eventually surrender are the cartwheel, the duckwalk, the backflip, the crab crawl, the headstand, the somersault, and hopscotch. Is it any wonder that by retirement, many of us have lost up to 75 percent of our ability to balance?

Runners take balance for granted until they're thrown off a treadmill or tumble nose-first onto a muddy path. Invariably, stunned faces arise from the spill. Watch a novice trail runner work terrain made perilous by loose footing: his stride turns to high, small steps and he lands farther forward on his toes to keep his body's center of gravity from sliding too far in any direction, thus making recovery easier in the event of a slip. He's compensating for—rather than using his muscles for—balance. This works in most cases, but it squanders speed and energy.

To be sure, trail running is a superb way to improve your balance, thanks to the delightful challenges it forces you to negotiate pell-mell. Even street running develops stabilizer muscles and proprioceptors, the nerve endings that detect changes in your body's position. In fact, *any* movement that repetitively shifts your center of gravity helps you build balance—but only within that range of movement. The problem for runners pops up with uneven and slippery surfaces or toppled trash cans, wandering puppies, and other obstacles that break your normal stride and direction. Unless you've got the muscles, the reaction time, and the confidence to execute these sudden recovery maneuvers, injury awaits.

If you feel smug about your gift for balance, as most of us do, try this: lift your right leg high behind you, then bend over and touch your left foot with your right hand. Now very slowly stand up straight, maintaining your body's full weight on one leg. Do 15 repetitions of this exercise on each foot. Even competitive runners will feel an ache in foot muscles that play only a supporting role in their regular workouts. Also notice that the most difficult part of this exercise is in merely standing up, since small flexes in your foot muscles can send your upper body tottering. Most of us wobble so badly, we make dancers and gymnasts smirk.

Balance is the transfer of forces and counterforces; its secret lies in movement. For runners, it matters not only how you strike the ground and shift your weight with each stride, but also how you absorb the impact. Runners with good balance barely slow for ice or mud because they transfer their weight so evenly that when a foot slips, they're already launched into the next step. Those who include stability training in their workouts know that balance makes you agile. It makes you fast.

You'll find dozens of ways to go about this type of training, from yoga and dance to weight training on balance balls. Pull out your unicycle. Learn to walk the tightrope. Any challenging movement that uses your whole body will help you rebuild neglected muscles along with the confidence that springs from good balance. Stability training is about learning to trust your body's innate gyroscope. It helps you spend more time on your feet, less time on your fanny.

"This may not be my fastest marathon, but it will be my most special."
—MARK BUCIAK, ON RUNNING HIS 27TH BOSTON MARATHON
11 WEEKS AFTER OPEN-HEART SURGERY

MONDAY, OCTOBER 27   301

WHERE & WHEN _____ DISTANCE _____
COMMENTS _____

TUESDAY, OCTOBER 28   302

WHERE & WHEN _____ DISTANCE _____
COMMENTS _____

WEDNESDAY, OCTOBER 29   303

WHERE & WHEN _____ DISTANCE _____
COMMENTS _____

THURSDAY, OCTOBER 30   304

WHERE & WHEN _____ DISTANCE _____
COMMENTS _____

FRIDAY, OCTOBER 31   305

WHERE & WHEN _____ DISTANCE _____
COMMENTS _____

WHERE & WHEN _____ DISTANCE _____

COMMENTS _____

SUNDAY, NOVEMBER 2

307

WHERE & WHEN _____ DISTANCE _____

COMMENTS _____

Physically active people have up to a 60 percent lower risk of
Alzheimer's than sedentary people.

DISTANCE THIS WEEK _____ WEIGHT_____

"If you're going through hell, keep going."　　　　　—WINSTON CHURCHILL

MONDAY, NOVEMBER 3　　　　　308

WHERE & WHEN _____ DISTANCE _____
COMMENTS _____

TUESDAY, NOVEMBER 4　　　　　309

WHERE & WHEN _____ DISTANCE _____
COMMENTS _____

WEDNESDAY, NOVEMBER 5　　　　　310

WHERE & WHEN _____ DISTANCE _____
COMMENTS _____

THURSDAY, NOVEMBER 6　　　　　311

WHERE & WHEN _____ DISTANCE _____
COMMENTS _____

FRIDAY, NOVEMBER 7　　　　　312

WHERE & WHEN _____ DISTANCE _____
COMMENTS _____

SATURDAY, NOVEMBER 8

WHERE & WHEN _____ DISTANCE _____
COMMENTS _____

SUNDAY, NOVEMBER 9

WHERE & WHEN _____ DISTANCE _____
COMMENTS _____

DISTANCE THIS WEEK _____ WEIGHT_____

"I'm a night runner. I don't want to see how far I have to go. And I like to have the street to myself." —JEFF CORWIN, HOST OF *CORWIN'S QUEST*

MONDAY, NOVEMBER 10   315

WHERE & WHEN _____ DISTANCE _____
COMMENTS _____

TUESDAY, NOVEMBER 11   316

WHERE & WHEN _____ DISTANCE _____
COMMENTS _____

WEDNESDAY, NOVEMBER 12   317

WHERE & WHEN _____ DISTANCE _____
COMMENTS _____

THURSDAY, NOVEMBER 13   318

WHERE & WHEN _____ DISTANCE _____
COMMENTS _____

FRIDAY, NOVEMBER 14   319

WHERE & WHEN _____ DISTANCE _____
COMMENTS _____

WHERE & WHEN _____ DISTANCE _____

COMMENTS _____

WHERE & WHEN _____ DISTANCE _____

COMMENTS _____

Unless your feet truly need motion-control shoes for
overpronation, don't get them; they can do more harm
than good.

DISTANCE THIS WEEK _____ WEIGHT _____

"It's the road signs: BEWARE OF LIONS."
—KIP LAGAT, KENYAN DISTANCE RUNNER, EXPLAINING WHY
HIS COUNTRY PRODUCES SO MANY GREAT RUNNERS

MONDAY, NOVEMBER 17   322

WHERE & WHEN _____ DISTANCE _____
COMMENTS _____

TUESDAY, NOVEMBER 18   323

WHERE & WHEN _____ DISTANCE _____
COMMENTS _____

WEDNESDAY, NOVEMBER 19   324

WHERE & WHEN _____ DISTANCE _____
COMMENTS _____

THURSDAY, NOVEMBER 20   325

WHERE & WHEN _____ DISTANCE _____
COMMENTS _____

FRIDAY, NOVEMBER 21   326

WHERE & WHEN _____ DISTANCE _____
COMMENTS _____

WHERE & WHEN _____ DISTANCE _____

COMMENTS _____

WHERE & WHEN _____ DISTANCE _____

COMMENTS _____

"When I'm doing hills, I say to myself, 'I love the hill, I love the hill.'
It helps."
                                        —SHAWN COLVIN, SINGER-SONGWRITER

MONDAY, NOVEMBER 24   329

WHERE & WHEN _____ DISTANCE _____
COMMENTS _____

TUESDAY, NOVEMBER 25   330

WHERE & WHEN _____ DISTANCE _____
COMMENTS _____

WEDNESDAY, NOVEMBER 26   331

WHERE & WHEN _____ DISTANCE _____
COMMENTS _____

THURSDAY, NOVEMBER 27   332

WHERE & WHEN _____ DISTANCE _____
COMMENTS _____

FRIDAY, NOVEMBER 28   333

WHERE & WHEN _____ DISTANCE _____
COMMENTS _____

SATURDAY, NOVEMBER 29

WHERE & WHEN _____ DISTANCE _____

COMMENTS _____

SUNDAY, NOVEMBER 30

WHERE & WHEN _____ DISTANCE _____

COMMENTS _____

DECEMBER

S	M	T	W	T	F	S
	1	2	3	4	5	6
7	8	9	10	11	12	13
14	15	16	17	18	19	20
21	22 HANUKKAH	23	24	25 CHRISTMAS DAY	26 BOXING DAY (CANADA)	27
28	29	30	31			

December: Victory

Even if numbers don't lie, common decency would let us *embellish* a little. This is the trouble with training logs. As you pore over the numbers you've recorded during the past year, notice how your eye lingers on the weeks, sometimes the months, in which you failed to meet your goals. Athletes tend to stare at defeat as through a cruel but hopeful window. Yet the year's end provides a splendid opportunity to toss out your prejudices about defeat and victory.

We all know that consistent training, for example, delivers the best results. But it doesn't deliver *consistent* results. Olympians and world-class marathoners will tell you as much. Any good training program should proceed with the understanding that you can't—and shouldn't—work at 100 percent around the calendar. Certainly you want to understand why dedication and desire wane, especially for extended periods. But instead of resolving to work through these dips with greater determination, resolve to reexamine your goals. Training reveals palpable truths about who you are; goals are abstractions. Let your goals realign with your truths, not the other way around.

While you're at it, make a promise to reinvest fun into your workouts and be willing to apply the imagination that makes this happen. Trail running, cross training, and partners (including the furry types that run on four feet) can jolt new life into a training program. So can a stopwatch or a racing registration form. Running might be the last place in our lives in which we get to invent the rules—all of them. Fun is a way of taking charge of your program.

Likewise, be fair in levying blame. It's astounding how many runners upbraid themselves for getting the flu or for pulling a hamstring. All runners eventually get sidelined. Work and family will always make demands on your training time, and the balancing act that modern life requires is rarely neat or comfortable. Remind yourself that running is less a claim on your time than a way of achieving better balance in the rest of your life. But also be aware that when the furnace breaks, the dog swallows a golf ball, or a deadline looms, your workout is a practical sacrifice, no blame necessary.

Meanwhile, are you learning the right lessons from a training slump? The things that dump you into a slump matter less than the things that bring you out. Look for patterns. Failed romances, career changes, or financial windfalls and setbacks can send you in either direction. These tell you very little. Far more important are the subtle signs you get from daily workouts. Boredom and joy are great signposts because every workout contains a little of both. Pay attention to how they change over time.

Finally, take a hard look at the things a training log can't tell you. The benefits to your long-term health, your ability to manage stress, the time you get to spend alone with yourself and the open road—these are the things that keep a running program alive. They don't reveal themselves in numbers.

"Most mistakes in a race are made in the first two minutes, perhaps in the very first minute." —JACK DANIELS, EXERCISE PHYSIOLOGIST AND COACH

MONDAY, DECEMBER 1   336

WHERE & WHEN _____ DISTANCE _____

COMMENTS _____

TUESDAY, DECEMBER 2   337

WHERE & WHEN _____ DISTANCE _____

COMMENTS _____

WEDNESDAY, DECEMBER 3   338

WHERE & WHEN _____ DISTANCE _____

COMMENTS _____

THURSDAY, DECEMBER 4   339

WHERE & WHEN _____ DISTANCE _____

COMMENTS _____

FRIDAY, DECEMBER 5   340

WHERE & WHEN _____ DISTANCE _____

COMMENTS _____

_____

_____

_____

_____

WHERE & WHEN _____ DISTANCE _____

COMMENTS _____

_____

_____

_____

_____

_____

WHERE & WHEN _____ DISTANCE _____

COMMENTS _____

_____

Anxious about a big summer race? Run a winter event in
preparation. Camaraderie, rather than competition, tends to
fuel cold-weather events; it can allay your fears.

"A denial of one's wounds is like the denial of one's life—it ends in premature death. A life lived is one that not only looks at wounds but embraces them and follows them like road signs."

—JIM MACLAREN, AMPUTEE ATHLETE

MONDAY, DECEMBER 8 343

WHERE & WHEN _____ DISTANCE _____
COMMENTS _____

TUESDAY, DECEMBER 9 344

WHERE & WHEN _____ DISTANCE _____
COMMENTS _____

WEDNESDAY, DECEMBER 10 345

WHERE & WHEN _____ DISTANCE _____
COMMENTS _____

THURSDAY, DECEMBER 11 346

WHERE & WHEN _____ DISTANCE _____
COMMENTS _____

FRIDAY, DECEMBER 12 347

WHERE & WHEN _____ DISTANCE _____
COMMENTS _____

WHERE & WHEN _____ DISTANCE _____
COMMENTS _____

WHERE & WHEN _____ DISTANCE _____
COMMENTS _____

Think of a marathon as three races: a 10-miler, another
10-miler, then a 10K. It makes the distance psychologically
manageable.

DISTANCE THIS WEEK _____ WEIGHT _____

"What kind of geek goes out and runs in a cloudburst just before midnight on his honeymoon? Me, I guess. But probably many others, too. You know who you are."

—MARK WILL-WEBER, EDITOR OF *THE QUOTABLE RUNNER*

MONDAY, DECEMBER 15   350

WHERE & WHEN _____ DISTANCE _____
COMMENTS _____

TUESDAY, DECEMBER 16   351

WHERE & WHEN _____ DISTANCE _____
COMMENTS _____

WEDNESDAY, DECEMBER 17   352

WHERE & WHEN _____ DISTANCE _____
COMMENTS _____

THURSDAY, DECEMBER 18   353

WHERE & WHEN _____ DISTANCE _____
COMMENTS _____

FRIDAY, DECEMBER 19   354

WHERE & WHEN _____ DISTANCE _____
COMMENTS _____

SATURDAY, DECEMBER 20

WHERE & WHEN _____ DISTANCE _____

COMMENTS _____

SUNDAY, DECEMBER 21

WHERE & WHEN _____ DISTANCE _____

COMMENTS _____

DISTANCE THIS WEEK _____ WEIGHT _____

DISTANCE CARRIED FORWARD _____

*"Running gave me the foundation from which to remember that
on day 67 of an expedition—while pulling a heavy sled across
Antarctica—it's about putting one foot in front of the other."*

—ANN BANCROFT, ARCTIC EXPLORER

MONDAY, DECEMBER 22   357

WHERE & WHEN _____ DISTANCE _____
COMMENTS _____

TUESDAY, DECEMBER 23   358

WHERE & WHEN _____ DISTANCE _____
COMMENTS _____

WEDNESDAY, DECEMBER 24   359

WHERE & WHEN _____ DISTANCE _____
COMMENTS _____

THURSDAY, DECEMBER 25   360

WHERE & WHEN _____ DISTANCE _____
COMMENTS _____

FRIDAY, DECEMBER 26   361

WHERE & WHEN _____ DISTANCE _____
COMMENTS _____

_____
_____
_____
_____

WHERE & WHEN _____ DISTANCE _____
COMMENTS _____
_____

_____
_____
_____

WHERE & WHEN _____ DISTANCE _____
COMMENTS _____
_____

Avoid sidewalks when possible. Concrete is significantly
harder on joints and connective tissue than asphalt,
grass, dirt, or mud.

DISTANCE THIS WEEK _____ WEIGHT_____

"It takes a long time to run around the world, so you see things on a small, personal scale. You see that the differences and distances between us are not as great as they appear on maps and in the media."
—JESPER OLSEN, ON COMPLETING A 22-MONTH RUN AROUND THE GLOBE

MONDAY, DECEMBER 29 — 364

WHERE & WHEN _____ DISTANCE _____
COMMENTS _____

TUESDAY, DECEMBER 30 — 365

WHERE & WHEN _____ DISTANCE _____
COMMENTS _____

WEDNESDAY, DECEMBER 31 — 366

WHERE & WHEN _____ DISTANCE _____
COMMENTS _____

THURSDAY, JANUARY 1 — 1

WHERE & WHEN _____ DISTANCE _____
COMMENTS _____

FRIDAY, JANUARY 2 — 2

WHERE & WHEN _____ DISTANCE _____
COMMENTS _____

WHERE & WHEN _____ DISTANCE _____
COMMENTS _____

WHERE & WHEN _____ DISTANCE _____
COMMENTS _____

Once you have a race strategy, put it out of your mind until
the starting gun. Overthinking it just spikes your anxiety.

Twelve Months of Running

DEC. 31	JAN. 7	JAN. 14	JAN. 21	JAN. 28	FEB. 4	FEB. 11	FEB. 18	FEB. 25	MARCH 3	MARCH 10	MARCH 17	MARCH 24

To create a cumulative bar graph of weekly mileage, apply an appropriate scale at the left-hand margin. Then fill in the bar for each week of running.

MARCH 31	APRIL 7	APRIL 14	APRIL 21	APRIL 28	MAY 5	MAY 12	MAY 19	MAY 26	JUNE 2	JUNE 9	JUNE 16	JUNE 23

To create a cumulative bar graph of weekly mileage, apply an appropriate scale at the left-hand margin. Then fill in the bar for each week of running.

	JUNE 30	JULY 7	JULY 14	JULY 21	JULY 28	AUG. 4	AUG. 11	AUG. 18	AUG. 25	SEPT. 1	SEPT. 8	SEPT. 15	SEPT. 22

To create a cumulative bar graph of weekly mileage, apply an appropriate scale at the left-hand margin. Then fill in the bar for each week of running.

SEPT. 29	OCT. 6	OCT. 13	OCT. 20	OCT. 27	NOV. 3	NOV. 10	NOV. 17	NOV. 24	DEC. 1	DEC. 8	DEC. 15	DEC. 22	DEC. 29

A Record of Races

DATE	PLACE	DISTANCE	TIME	PACE	COMMENTS AND EXCUSES

A Record of Races

DATE	PLACE	DISTANCE	TIME	PACE	COMMENTS AND EXCUSES

Marathon Quick Reference Split Times*

Mile	1	2	3	4	5	6	7	8	
PACE									PACE
2:04	4:44	9:28	14:11	18:55	23:39	28:23	33:07	37:50	2:04
2:05	4:46	9:32	14:18	19:08	23:51	28:37	33:23	38:09	2:05
2:06	4:48	9:36	14:26	19:14	24:03	28:51	33:40	38:29	2:06
2:07	4:51	9:42	14:33	19:24	24:15	29:06	33:57	38:48	2:07
2:08	4:53	9:48	14:40	19:34	24:27	29:20	34:14	39:07	2:08
2:09	4:55	9:50	14:46	19:41	24:36	29:31	34:26	39:21	2:09
2:10	4:58	9:55	14:53	19:50	24:48	29:46	34:43	39:41	2:10
2:11	5:00	10:00	15:00	20:00	25:00	30:00	35:00	40:00	2:11
2:12	5:02	10:04	15:06	20:12	25:14	30:16	35:18	40:20	2:12
2:13	5:05	10:10	15:14	20:19	25:24	30:29	35:34	40:38	2:13
2:14	5:07	10:13	15:20	20:26	25:33	30:40	35:46	40:53	2:14
2:15	5:09	10:18	15:27	20:36	25:45	30:54	36:03	41:12	2:15
2:16	5:11	10:23	15:34	20:46	25:57	31:08	36:20	41:31	2:16
2:17	5:14	10:28	15:41	20:55	26:09	31:23	36:37	41:50	2:17
2:18	5:16	10:32	15:49	21:05	26:21	31:37	36:53	42:10	2:18
2:19	5:18	10:36	15:54	21:12	26:30	31:48	37:06	42:24	2:19
2:20	5:21	10:41	16:01	21:22	26:42	32:02	37:23	42:43	2:20
2:21	5:23	10:46	16:09	21:31	26:54	32:17	37:40	43:02	2:21
2:22	5:25	10:50	16:16	21:41	27:06	32:31	37:56	43:22	2:22
2:23	5:28	10:55	16:23	21:50	27:18	32:46	38:13	43:41	2:23
2:24	5:30	11:00	16:30	22:00	27:30	33:00	38:30	44:00	2:24
2:25	5:32	11:04	16:35	22:07	27:39	33:11	38:43	44:14	2:25
2:26	5:34	11:08	16:42	22:17	27:51	33:25	38:59	44:34	2:26
2:27	5:37	11:13	16:50	22:26	28:03	33:40	39:16	44:53	2:27
2:28	5:39	11:18	16:57	22:36	28:15	33:54	39:33	45:12	2:28
2:29	5:41	11:23	17:04	22:46	28:27	34:08	39:50	45:31	2:29
2:30	5:44	11:28	17:11	22:55	28:39	34:23	40:07	45:50	2:30
2:35	5:55	11:50	17:46	23:41	29:36	35:31	41:26	47:22	2:35
2:40	6:07	12:13	18:20	24:26	30:33	36:40	42:46	48:53	2:40
2:45	6:18	12:36	18:54	25:12	31:30	37:48	44:06	50:24	2:45
2:50	6:29	12:59	19:28	25:58	32:27	38:56	45:26	51:55	2:50
2:55	6:41	13:22	20:02	26:43	33:24	40:05	46:46	53:26	2:55
3:00	6:52	13:44	20:37	27:29	34:21	41:23	48:05	54:58	3:00
3:15	7:26	14:53	22:19	29:46	37:12	44:38	52:05	59:52	3:15
3:30	8:01	16:02	24:04	32:05	40:06	48:07	56:08	1:04:10	3:30
3:45	8:35	17:11	25:46	34:22	42:57	51:32	1:00:08	1:08:43	3:45
4:00	9:10	18:19	27:29	36:38	45:48	54:57	1:04:07	1:13:17	4:00
4:15	9:44	19:28	29:11	38:55	48:39	58:23	1:08:07	1:17:50	4:15
4:30	10:18	20:36	30:54	41:12	51:30	1:01:48	1:12:06	1:22:24	4:30
4:45	10:53	21:46	32:38	43:31	54:24	1:05:17	1:16:10	1:27:02	4:45
5:00	11:27	22:54	34:21	45:48	57:15	1:08:42	1:20:09	1:31:36	5:00

*Times are rounded off to accommodate fractions of a second.

Mile	9	10	11	12	13	14	15	
PACE								PACE
2:04	42:34	47:18	52:02	56:46	1:01:29	1:06:13	1:10:57	2:04
2:05	42:56	47:42	52:28	57:14	1:02:06	1:06:52	1:11:36	2:05
2:06	43:17	48:06	52:55	57:43	1:02:32	1:07:20	1:12:09	2:06
2:07	43:39	48:30	53:21	58:12	1:03:03	1:07:54	1:12:45	2:07
2:08	44:00	48:54	53:47	58:41	1:03:11	1:08:27	1:13:30	2:08
2:09	44:17	49:12	54:07	59:02	1:03:58	1:08:53	1:13:48	2:09
2:10	44:38	49:36	54:34	59:31	1:04:29	1:09:26	1:14:24	2:10
2:11	45:00	50:00	55:00	1:00:00	1:05:00	1:10:00	1:15:00	2:11
2:12	45:22	50:24	55:26	1:00:28	1:05:30	1:10:32	1:15:34	2:12
2:13	45:43	50:48	55:53	1:00:58	1:06:02	1:11:07	1:16:12	2:13
2:14	46:00	51:06	56:13	1:01:19	1:06:26	1:11:32	1:16:39	2:14
2:15	46:21	51:30	56:39	1:01:48	1:06:57	1:12:06	1:17:15	2:15
2:16	46:43	51:54	57:05	1:02:17	1:07:28	1:12:40	1:17:51	2:16
2:17	47:04	52:18	57:32	1:02:46	1:08:00	1:13:13	1:18:27	2:17
2:18	47:26	52:42	57:58	1:03:14	1:08:31	1:13:47	1:19:03	2:18
2:19	47:42	53:00	58:18	1:03:36	1:08:54	1:14:12	1:19:30	2:19
2:20	48:04	53:24	58:44	1:04:05	1:09:25	1:14:46	1:20:06	2:20
2:21	48:25	53:48	59:11	1:04:34	1:09:56	1:15:19	1:20:42	2:21
2:22	48:47	54:12	59:37	1:05:02	1:10:28	1:15:53	1:21:18	2:22
2:23	49:08	54:36	1:00:04	1:05:31	1:10:59	1:16:26	1:21:54	2:23
2:24	49:30	55:00	1:00:30	1:06:00	1:11:30	1:17:00	1:22:30	2:24
2:25	49:46	55:18	1:00:50	1:06:22	1:11:53	1:17:25	1:22:57	2:25
2:26	50:08	55:42	1:01:16	1:06:50	1:12:25	1:17:59	1:23:33	2:26
2:27	50:29	56:06	1:01:42	1:07:19	1:12:56	1:18:32	1:24:09	2:27
2:28	50:51	56:30	1:02:09	1:07:48	1:13:27	1:19:06	1:24:45	2:28
2:29	51:13	56:54	1:02:35	1:08:17	1:13:58	1:19:40	1:25:21	2:29
2:30	51:34	57:18	1:03:02	1:08:46	1:14:47	1:20:13	1:25:57	2:30
2:35	53:17	59:12	1:05:07	1:11:02	1:16:58	1:22:53	1:28:48	2:35
2:40	54:59	1:01:06	1:07:13	1:13:19	1:19:26	1:25:32	1:31:39	2:40
2:45	56:42	1:03:00	1:09:18	1:15:36	1:21:54	1:28:12	1:34:30	2:45
2:50	58:25	1:04:54	1:11:23	1:17:53	1:24:22	1:30:52	1:37:21	2:50
2:55	1:00:07	1:06:48	1:13:29	1:20:10	1:26:50	1:33:31	1:40:12	2:55
3:00	1:01:50	1:08:42	1:15:34	1:22:26	1:29:19	1:36:11	1:43:03	3:00
3:15	1:06:58	1:14:24	1:21:50	1:29:17	1:36:43	1:44:10	1:51:36	3:15
3:30	1:12:11	1:20:12	1:28:13	1:36:14	1:44:16	1:52:17	2:00:18	3:30
3:45	1:17:19	1:25:54	1:34:29	1:43:05	1:51:40	2:00:16	2:08:51	3:45
4:00	1:22:26	1:31:36	1:40:46	1:49:55	1:59:05	2:08:14	2:17:24	4:00
4:15	1:27:34	1:37:18	1:47:02	1:56:46	2:06:29	2:16:13	2:25:57	4:15
4:30	1:32:42	1:43:00	1:53:18	2:03:36	2:13:54	2:24:12	2:34:30	4:30
4:45	1:37:55	1:48:48	1:59:41	2:10:34	2:21:26	2:32:19	2:43:12	4:45
5:00	1:43:03	1:54:30	2:05:57	2:17:24	2:28:51	2:40:18	2:51:45	5:00

*Times are rounded off to accommodate fractions of a second.

Mile	16	17	18	19	20	21	22	
PACE								PACE
2:04	1:15:41	1:20:25	1:25:08	1:29:52	1:34:36	1:39:20	1:44:04	2:04
2:05	1:16:19	1:21:05	1:25:51	1:30:37	1:35:24	1:40:10	1:44:56	2:05
2:06	1:16:58	1:21:46	1:26:35	1:31:23	1:36:12	1:41:06	1:45:49	2:06
2:07	1:17:36	1:22:27	1:27:18	1:32:09	1:37:00	1:41:51	1:46:42	2:07
2:08	1:18:14	1:23:08	1:28:12	1:32:55	1:37:48	1:42:41	1:47:35	2:08
2:09	1:18:43	1:23:38	1:28:34	1:33:29	1:38:24	1:43:19	1:48:14	2:09
2:10	1:19:22	1:24:19	1:29:17	1:34:14	1:39:12	1:44:10	1:49:07	2:10
2:11	1:20:00	1:25:00	1:30:00	1:35:00	1:40:00	1:45:00	1:50:00	2:11
2:12	1:20:36	1:25:38	1:30:40	1:35:42	1:40:46	1:45:48	1:50:50	2:12
2:13	1:21:17	1:26:22	1:31:26	1:36:31	1:41:36	1:46:41	1:51:46	2:13
2:14	1:21:46	1:26:52	1:31:58	1:37:05	1:42:12	1:47:19	1:52:25	2:14
2:15	1:22:24	1:27:33	1:32:42	1:37:51	1:43:00	1:48:09	1:53:18	2:15
2:16	1:23:02	1:28:14	1:33:25	1:38:37	1:43:48	1:48:59	1:54:11	2:16
2:17	1:23:41	1:28:55	1:34:08	1:39:22	1:44:36	1:49:50	1:55:04	2:17
2:18	1:24:19	1:29:35	1:34:52	1:40:08	1:45:24	1:50:40	1:55:56	2:18
2:19	1:24:48	1:30:06	1:35:24	1:40:42	1:46:00	1:51:18	1:56:36	2:19
2:20	1:25:26	1:30:47	1:36:07	1:41:28	1:46:48	1:52:08	1:57:29	2:20
2:21	1:26:05	1:31:28	1:36:50	1:42:13	1:47:36	1:52:59	1:58:22	2:21
2:22	1:26:43	1:32:08	1:37:34	1:42:59	1:48:24	1:53:49	1:59:14	2:22
2:23	1:27:22	1:32:49	1:38:17	1:43:44	1:49:12	1:54:40	2:00:07	2:23
2:24	1:28:00	1:33:30	1:39:00	1:44:30	1:50:00	1:55:30	2:01:00	2:24
2:25	1:28:29	1:34:06	1:39:32	1:45:04	1:50:36	1:56:08	2:01:40	2:25
2:26	1:29:07	1:34:41	1:40:16	1:45:50	1:51:24	1:56:58	2:02:32	2:26
2:27	1:29:46	1:35:22	1:40:59	1:46:35	1:52:12	1:57:49	2:03:25	2:27
2:28	1:30:24	1:36:03	1:41:42	1:47:21	1:53:00	1:58:39	2:04:18	2:28
2:29	1:31:02	1:36:44	1:42:25	1:48:07	1:53:48	1:59:29	2:05:11	2:29
2:30	1:31:41	1:37:25	1:43:08	1:48:52	1:54:36	2:00:20	2:06:04	2:30
2:35	1:34:43	1:40:38	1:46:34	1:52:29	1:58:24	2:04:19	2:10:14	2:35
2:40	1:37:46	1:43:52	1:49:59	1:56:05	2:02:12	2:08:19	2:14:25	2:40
2:45	1:40:48	1:47:06	1:53:24	1:59:42	2:06:00	2:12:18	2:18:36	2:45
2:50	1:43:50	1:50:20	1:56:49	2:03:19	2:09:48	2:16:17	2:22:47	2:50
2:55	1:46:53	1:53:34	2:00:14	2:06:55	2:13:36	2:20:17	2:26:58	2:55
3:00	1:49:55	1:56:47	2:03:40	2:10:32	2:17:24	2:24:16	2:31:08	3:00
3:15	1:59:02	2:06:29	2:13:55	2:21:22	2:28:48	2:36:14	2:43:41	3:15
3:30	2:08:19	2:16:20	2:24:22	2:32:23	2:40:24	2:48:25	2:56:26	3:30
3:45	2:17:26	2:26:02	2:34:37	2:43:13	2:51:48	3:00:23	3:08:59	3:45
4:00	2:26:34	2:35:43	2:44:53	2:54:02	3:03:12	3:12:22	3:21:31	4:00
4:15	2:35:41	2:45:25	2:55:08	3:04:52	3:14:36	3:24:20	3:34:04	4:15
4:30	2:44:48	2:55:06	3:05:24	3:15:42	3:26:00	3:36:18	3:44:24	4:30
4:45	2:54:05	3:05:58	3:15:50	3:26:43	3:37:36	3:48:29	3:59:22	4:45
5:00	3:03:12	3:14:39	3:26:06	3:37:33	3:49:00	4:00:27	4:11:54	5:00

*Times are rounded off to accommodate fractions of a second.

Mile	23	24	25	26	26.2	PACE
PACE						
2:04	1:48:47	1:53:31	1:58:15	2:02:59	2:03:56	2:04
2:05	1:49:42	1:54:29	1:59:15	2:04:12	2:04:58	2:05
2:06	1:50:38	1:55:26	2:00:15	2:05:06	2:06:00	2:06
2:07	1:51:32	1:56:23	2:01:14	2:06:05	2:07:00	2:07
2:08	1:52:27	1:57:21	2:02:14	2:07:06	2:08:00	2:08
2:09	1:53:10	1:58:05	2:03:00	2:07:55	2:08:55	2:09
2:10	1:54:05	1:59:02	2:04:00	2:08:57	2:09:57	2:10
2:11	1:55:00	2:00:00	2:05:00	2:10:00	2:11:00	2:11
2:12	1:55:52	2:00:54	2:05:56	2:11:02	2:12:00	2:12
2:13	1:56:48	2:01:50	2:06:55	2:12:00	2:13:00	2:13
2:14	1:57:32	2:02:38	2:07:45	2:12:52	2:13:53	2:14
2:15	1:58:27	2:03:36	2:08:45	2:13:54	2:14:56	2:15
2:16	1:59:22	2:04:34	2:09:45	2:14:56	2:15:59	2:16
2:17	2:00:17	2:05:31	2:10:43	2:15:57	2:17:00	2:17
2:18	2:01:13	2:06:28	2:11:42	2:16:55	2:18:00	2:18
2:19	2:01:54	2:07:12	2:12:30	2:17:48	2:18:58	2:19
2:20	2:02:49	2:08:10	2:13:30	2:18:50	2:19:55	2:20
2:21	2:03:44	2:09:07	2:14:30	2:19:53	2:20:57	2:21
2:22	2:04:40	2:10:05	2:15:30	2:20:55	2:22:00	2:22
2:23	2:05:35	2:11:02	2:16:30	2:21:58	2:23:00	2:23
2:24	2:06:30	2:12:00	2:17:30	2:23:00	2:24:00	2:24
2:25	2:07:11	2:12:43	2:18:15	2:23:47	2:24:53	2:25
2:26	2:08:07	2:13:41	2:19:15	2:24:49	2:25:56	2:26
2:27	2:09:02	2:14:38	2:20:15	2:25:52	2:26:59	2:27
2:28	2:09:57	2:15:36	2:21:15	2:26:54	2:28:00	2:28
2:29	2:10:52	2:16:34	2:22:15	2:27:56	2:29:00	2:29
2:30	2:11:46	2:17:28	2:23:12	2:28:55	2:30:00	2:30
2:35	2:16:10	2:22:05	2:28:00	2:33:55	2:35:00	2:35
2:40	2:20:32	2:26:38	2:32:42	2:38:48	2:40:00	2:40
2:45	2:24:54	2:31:12	2:37:30	2:43:48	2:45:00	2:45
2:50	2:29:16	2:35:46	2:42:15	2:48:44	2:50:00	2:50
2:55	2:33:38	2:40:19	2:47:00	2:53:41	2:55:00	2:55
3:00	2:38:06	2:44:53	2:51:45	2:58:37	3:00:00	3:00
3:15	2:51:07	2:58:34	3:06:00	3:13:26	3:15:00	3:15
3:30	3:04:28	3:12:29	3:20:30	3:28:31	3:30:00	3:30
3:45	3:17:34	3:26:10	3:34:45	3:43:20	3:45:00	3:45
4:00	3:30:41	3:39:50	3:49:00	3:58:10	4:00:00	4:00
4:15	3:43:47	3:53:31	4:03:15	4:12:59	4:15:00	4:15
4:30	3:56:54	4:07:12	4:17:30	4:27:48	4:30:00	4:30
4:45	4:10:14	4:21:07	4:32:00	4:42:53	4:45:00	4:45
5:00	4:23:21	4:47:48	4:46:15	4:57:42	5:00:00	5:00

*Times are rounded off to accommodate fractions of a second.

2008

JANUARY

S	M	T	W	T	F	S
		1	2	3	4	5
6	7	8	9	10	11	12
13	14	15	16	17	18	19
20	21	22	23	24	25	26
27	28	29	30	31		

FEBRUARY

S	M	T	W	T	F	S
					1	2
3	4	5	6	7	8	9
10	11	12	13	14	15	16
17	18	19	20	21	22	23
24	25	26	27	28	29	

MARCH

S	M	T	W	T	F	S
						1
2	3	4	5	6	7	8
9	10	11	12	13	14	15
16	17	18	19	20	21	22
23/30	24/31	25	26	27	28	29

APRIL

S	M	T	W	T	F	S
		1	2	3	4	5
6	7	8	9	10	11	12
13	14	15	16	17	18	19
20	21	22	23	24	25	26
27	28	29	30			

MAY

S	M	T	W	T	F	S
				1	2	3
4	5	6	7	8	9	10
11	12	13	14	15	16	17
18	19	20	21	22	23	24
25	26	27	28	29	30	31

JUNE

S	M	T	W	T	F	S
1	2	3	4	5	6	7
8	9	10	11	12	13	14
15	16	17	18	19	20	21
22	23	24	25	26	27	28
29	30					

JULY

S	M	T	W	T	F	S
		1	2	3	4	5
6	7	8	9	10	11	12
13	14	15	16	17	18	19
20	21	22	23	24	25	26
27	28	29	30	31		

AUGUST

S	M	T	W	T	F	S
					1	2
3	4	5	6	7	8	9
10	11	12	13	14	15	16
17	18	19	20	21	22	23
24/31	25	26	27	28	29	30

SEPTEMBER

S	M	T	W	T	F	S
	1	2	3	4	5	6
7	8	9	10	11	12	13
14	15	16	17	18	19	20
21	22	23	24	25	26	27
28	29	30				

OCTOBER

S	M	T	W	T	F	S
			1	2	3	4
5	6	7	8	9	10	11
12	13	14	15	16	17	18
19	20	21	22	23	24	25
26	27	28	29	30	31	

NOVEMBER

S	M	T	W	T	F	S
						1
2	3	4	5	6	7	8
9	10	11	12	13	14	15
16	17	18	19	20	21	22
23/30	24	25	26	27	28	29

DECEMBER

S	M	T	W	T	F	S
	1	2	3	4	5	6
7	8	9	10	11	12	13
14	15	16	17	18	19	20
21	22	23	24	25	26	27
28	29	30	31			

2009

JANUARY

S	M	T	W	T	F	S
				1	2	3
4	5	6	7	8	9	10
11	12	13	14	15	16	17
18	19	20	21	22	23	24
25	26	27	28	29	30	31

FEBRUARY

S	M	T	W	T	F	S
1	2	3	4	5	6	7
8	9	10	11	12	13	14
15	16	17	18	19	20	21
22	23	24	25	26	27	28

MARCH

S	M	T	W	T	F	S
1	2	3	4	5	6	7
8	9	10	11	12	13	14
15	16	17	18	19	20	21
22	23	24	25	26	27	28
29	30	31				

APRIL

S	M	T	W	T	F	S
		1	2	3	4	
5	6	7	8	9	10	11
12	13	14	15	16	17	18
19	20	21	22	23	24	25
26	27	28	29	30		

MAY

S	M	T	W	T	F	S
					1	2
3	4	5	6	7	8	9
10	11	12	13	14	15	16
17	18	19	20	21	22	23
24/31	25	26	27	28	29	30

JUNE

S	M	T	W	T	F	S
	1	2	3	4	5	6
7	8	9	10	11	12	13
14	15	16	17	18	19	20
21	22	23	24	25	26	27
28	29	30				

JULY

S	M	T	W	T	F	S
		1	2	3	4	
5	6	7	8	9	10	11
12	13	14	15	16	17	18
19	20	21	22	23	24	25
26	27	28	29	30	31	

AUGUST

S	M	T	W	T	F	S
						1
2	3	4	5	6	7	8
9	10	11	12	13	14	15
16	17	18	19	20	21	22
23/30	24/31	25	26	27	28	29

SEPTEMBER

S	M	T	W	T	F	S
		1	2	3	4	5
6	7	8	9	10	11	12
13	14	15	16	17	18	19
20	21	22	23	24	25	26
27	28	29	30			

OCTOBER

S	M	T	W	T	F	S
		1	2	3		
4	5	6	7	8	9	10
11	12	13	14	15	16	17
18	19	20	21	22	23	24
25	26	27	28	29	30	31

NOVEMBER

S	M	T	W	T	F	S
1	2	3	4	5	6	7
8	9	10	11	12	13	14
15	16	17	18	19	20	21
22	23	24	25	26	27	28
29	30					

DECEMBER

S	M	T	W	T	F	S
		1	2	3	4	5
6	7	8	9	10	11	12
13	14	15	16	17	18	19
20	21	22	23	24	25	26
27	28	29	30	31		